Here & H

Here & Human

An anthology of contemporary verse

compiled by F E S Finn

John Murray
50 Albemarle Street London

Photoset, printed and bound
in Great Britain by
REDWOOD BURN LIMITED
Trowbridge & Esher

0 7195 3291 4 School
0 7195 3306 6 Paperback

Contents

ANTHONY THWAITE *(cont'd)*

Illustrations

Patricia Beer

Author's Introduction

The poems presented here cover nearly twenty years of my writing life. 'Ghost' was one of my very early poems. I wrote it after my father's funeral, in the mid-Fifties. Though his death was certainly the impetus behind the poem, there is not a great deal in it that is specifically about him and it might well seem to be a general reflection on the influence which relatives and close friends can exert even after death on those who are still alive. I have written much more precisely about my father, and indeed more precisely about most subjects, since then. A poem in *The Estuary*, which appeared in 1971, concerns him very directly. He was a railwayman all his working life. 'One Man One Vote' describes a dilemma he solved – bravely, I think – in his old age, when his loyalty to the railway and his loyalty to the Plymouth Brethren sect, of which he was a member, came into conflict. He did not live to see the closing of the track from Sidmouth Junction to Exmouth, but I have celebrated its passing in 'The Branch Line'; we knew and loved this line in childhood and, because of my father's job, felt an almost proprietorial interest in it.

Several of the poems in this selection illustrate the supreme importance of childhood feelings and experiences when it comes to writing poetry in adult life, though there usually has to be a second experience to activate the first. 'Summer Song for me and my Aunts', in *Just like the Resurrection* 1963, is an example of this. (The title comes from *The Winter's Tale*, by the way.) I wrote the poem after a visit to Haworth Parsonage where I had been greatly moved by all the sad relics of the Brontës. I doubt if this visit would have been enough in itself for a poem; what really precipitated it was the deeper reality of my youthful dread of getting consumption myself. It was a disease rampant in those days and in fact a great many of my mother's relatives had died of it, as had, of course, the Brontës. 'The Estuary' is another poem which though written recently is actually based on a bereavement – my mother's death – which happened when I was fourteen but which I was not able to face till much later. What enabled me to do so, in life and in poetry, was contemplation of the geographical place – the estuary of the Exe – which symbolized the change from happiness to unhappiness.

Yet another poem which springs essentially from a childhood preoccupation is 'Arms' (*The Estuary*). As the last verse describes, my great-grandfather, who was Master of a brig called the *Magyar*, went down with his ship, clasping in his arms his eldest son, a boy who had gone on the voyage with him. I heard this story when I was very young and it made a great impression on me. But when I came to write this poem, in middle-age, a great many other things had come into the picture, such as the loss of religious faith.

But childhood of course is not the only inspiration. These poems suggest a cross-section of the many occasions which can stimulate any of us into verse. Any happening in everyday life can do it: reading the newspaper ('Four Years After'); visiting an art gallery abroad ('Picture of Workers Resting'); visiting the Natural History Museum in South Kensington ('Female, Extinct'); happily waiting for the family to arrive at Christmas ('Christmas Eve'). The poem which I have felt easiest with recently and one which has proved most popular is a perfectly factual, autobiographical account of what happened to me last year when I went on down to the country to open up the house before the others arrived. It is called 'After Death' and will appear in a new collection, *Driving West*, very soon. I hope you will like the illustration in this anthology; it captures exactly the panic and deadly frustration which I imagine the trapped bird must have felt.

GHOST

He died a year ago
And months of quiet have made
Him tall as air

Whose speech was like a root
Groping and grey. Each sun
Tolls him awake.

He was enclosed in wood,
Hushed into crumbling; smooth
Graining of ribs

Showed where the life had lain.
The sawing light caught no more
On knotted blood.

But he escaped through paths
Of soil and worm and stone
To fidget like a tree

Over this house, and all
The leaves that flew are tamed
On to his hand.

AFTER DEATH

Opening up the house
After three weeks away
I found bird droppings
All over the ground floor,
White and heavy on the windows,
On the worktop,
On the cupboards,
On every wild hope of freedom.

I could not find any bird
At first, and feared
Some science fiction mystery,

To be horribly explained,
As soon as whatever
It was felt sure
It had got me alone,
A mile from the village.

At last I discovered him,
Weightless and out of the running,
More null than old wrapping paper
A month after Christmas.
No food inside him, of course,
He had died of hunger
And no waste either,
He was quite empty.

His desperate ghost
Flew down my throat and my ears.
There was no air
He had not suffered in.
He lay in one place,
His droppings were everywhere,
More vivid, more terrible
Than he had been, ever.

FEMALE, EXTINCT

Her ribcage is eked out
With bits of wire.
Her bony gloves
Have no marrow in them.

You can take her home
On a postcard
Separately. She once
Stood up with hundreds

As if to bellow
The Hallelujah Chorus.
Her voice fell
Forward into the mud.

Her sons, little dragons,
All lumbered away.
Her skull was probably
Left out for seasons

In a far pasture
Or on a battlefield
To be gathered up
By wilier beings.

The air of the museum
Snuffles in her nose.
Her passionate jaws
Shout 'Give me time.'

THE KILLING OF SPARROWS

I see nothing of the killing of sparrows.
They are laid out on the kitchen floor,
Presents from the killer,
Or so the cat books say.

I looked long and closely at the first.
In death it was full of surprises:
Its beak huge, the only part of it
That was not already shrinking.
More grey feathers than I realized
A sparrow had. Beadiness gone
A prophetic look about its eyes.
Claws changed from movement to gesture.

Secondhand murder.
I indulge the killer.

I look more casually now.
Bigger as the cat grows, as the year goes on,
The dead birds tick and chime
The cat's life away, mine
And the strength of the town house.

THE CLOCK

The oldest clock we have
Stops every few days.
The weights catch on the case
And do not go right down.

It has the appearance
Of any eight-day clock.
We respect its size, not
Winding it like a watch.

The relative who gave
It to us used to say
A stopped clock foretells death,
Not thinking us so rash.

We have refuted this
Already, but it is
So easy to hear death
In the silence of stairs

Where once a pendulum
Thudded like a cart-horse
That now a deep meadow
Has swallowed, you can see

How some poets, like Donne,
Have 'used themselves in jest
By feigned deaths to die',
A run-through for the dark,

A drill. Obviously
Death cannot come each time
The clock stops. It may be
Good practice to think so.

ABBEY TOMB

I told them not to ring the bells
The night the Vikings came
Out of the sea and passed us by.
The fog was thick as cream

And in the abbey we stood still
As if our breath might blare
Or pulses rattle if we once
Stopped staring at the door.

Through the walls and through the fog
We heard them passing by.
The deafer monks thanked God too soon
And later only I
Could catch the sound of prowling men
Still present in the hills
So everybody else agreed
To ring the abbey bells.

And even while the final clang
Still snored upon the air,
And while the ringers joked their way
Down round the spiral stair,
Before the spit of fervent prayer
Had dried into the stone
The raiders came back through the fog
And killed us one by one.

Father Abbot at the altar
Lay back with his knees
Doubled under him, caught napping
In the act of praise.
Brother John lay unresponsive
In the warming room.
The spiders came out for the heat
And then the rats for him.

Under the level of the sheep
Who graze here all the time
We lie now, under tourists' feet
Who in good weather come.
I told them not to ring the bells
But centuries of rain
And blustering have made their tombs
Look just as right as mine.

ARMS

I was brought up to believe
In the Everlasting Arms
And took comfort for some years
In the fatherly muscle
And grip, but fell out of them
Gradually and in slow
Motion as God dissolved. Fell
Into nightmares about arms

And specially one picture
Of the world lying flooded
With all the animals drowned,
Visible still in one foot
Of water, frozen, never
To wriggle with the tide or
Rustle to pieces. Stiff-legged
The sheep who could not embrace

And flex as the lions could
Nevertheless lay in their
Ramrod protectiveness
Holding each other like bars.
These limbs were not immortal
And, perishing, they woke me
As in a story I heard:
When my grandfather went down

With his brig in the North Sea
On a calm clear evening
There was no wireless to send
Last love on. He put his arms
Round his son and there he stood,
Protector, up to his knees
In death, and that was the last
That anyone saw of him.

CONCERT AT LONG MELFORD CHURCH

For Jane Lowenstein

Long Melford church is built of flint and glass,
The tombstones make your teeth ache
And the paths leading up to it look
Particularly hard through so much soft grass.

Today a concert in afternoon light
Gives the church a more brittle purpose
Than usual, more capable of close.
From this people will go home free tonight.

And there are so many. A Suffolk Festival
Has brought everybody out from London
Like a saint or a marvel. The proportion
Of living men to graves is medieval.

We were taught not to walk on graves as children.
Holding flowers for grandparents, we worked out
Where each corpse would be, walked round it,
Steering past the heels, elbow and chin

Of those submerged and dangerous bodies.
But today the paths and the narrow porch
Cannot contain those coming out of church
During the interval, into the sun and yew trees.

They spread all over the churchyard. They scan
The crowd, recognize, smile and shake hands.
By each tombstone a well-dressed person stands.
It looks just like the Resurrection.

THE BRANCH LINE

One train was the last.
Decorated with a crowd
Of people who like last things,
Not normally travellers,
Mostly children and their fathers,
It left to a theatrical blast
As the guard for once played
At his job, with mixed feelings.

Photographers were there,
For the only time perhaps
Since the railway groped
Down into these shires
First of all, and the squires
Fretted about their deer.
There were flags and a few maps,
And cheers as the signal dropped.

The platform is now old
And empty, but still shows
The act of waiting.
Beyond it the meadows,
Where once the toy shadows
Of funnel and smoke bowled,
Are pure green, and no echoes
Squeeze into the cutting.

The villages that gave
The stations their names
Were always out of sight,
Behind a hill, up a lane,
Dead, except when a train
Fetched somebody forth alive.
But now no one at all comes
Out of them by this route.

The level-crossing gates
Guard passers-by from nothing
Now. The railway's bite
Is dislocated by time,
Too out-of-date to harm
Like a gummy old cat's.
The road is the frightening
Power, the current favourite.

If the particular fast
Bright dragon of childhood
Is null, I feel the same,
Extinct; not obsolete
Nor dead, but lightweight.
The line has left no ghost
Even, but is as void
As my discarded name.

My past has been defaced
Because it ran together
So often with this line.
Trains exist elsewhere
But different, sinister:
Heads, looking out for a last
Good-bye, freeze and weather
To the sky, as at Tyburn.

THE ESTUARY

A light elegant wall waves down
The riverside, for tidiness
Or decoration – this water
Needs little keeping in – but turns
The corner to face the ocean
And thickens to a bastion.

No one can really taste or smell
Where the salt starts but at one point
The first building looks out to sea
And the two sides of the river
Are forced apart by cold light
And wind and different grasses.

I see this now, but at one time
I had to believe that the two
Sides were almost identical.
I was a child who dared not seem
Gloomy. Traversing grey water
From the east side where I was born

And had spent a normal cross life,
To live gratefully with strangers
On the west side, I grinned and clowned.
I did not go back for ages
And became known for cheerfulness
In a house where all was not well.

Grief was a poltergeist that would
Not materialize but broke
Everything. Neither believed in
Nor dreaded, it took one decade
To appear, one to be recognized,
Then cleared the air wonderfully

So that nowadays I am able
To see the estuary as two
Distinct pieces of countryside,
Not a great deal to choose between
Them perhaps but at least different,
Rising normally from two roots.

On one bank stiff fields of corn grow
To the hilltop, are draped over
It surrealistically.
On the other, little white boats
Sag sideways twice every day
As the sea pulls away their prop.

SUMMER SONG FOR ME AND MY AUNTS

Never forget the moors
Behind the house, never
Let being a woman
Or the baking of bread
Or sizing up a sermon

Keep you off the heath
And far from the stone wall
That is no more than gauze
To these strong winds.
Headaches come indoors.

Walk uphill from the house
And the graves already there.
The chill of waterfalls
Cannot cause worse coughing
Than sprig-papered walls

Where you die in turn
On a narrow sofa
Boxed up from the storm.
Dying women can walk
On the moors without harm.

ARMISTICE DAY

As I was going to work that morning
I saw the flag at half mast
And remembered individual death,
A young cousin who choked, a grandfather
Who rattled all night like snoring
And several others.

I did not ask for some time
'Who?'
Being afraid to know
To hear someone's name.

It was Armistice Day
So I was finally told.

Why ever did I say: 'What a relief,
I thought somebody was dead.'
For I remember plural death
As well as singular,
The red mutilated sky over Plymouth
And in the moorland towns
The ambulance men standing by all night
And several other incidents.

ONE MAN ONE VOTE

My railwayman father voted
Only once in his entire life.
Politics was for the children
Of this present world and not for
Those who were marching to Zion.

He would not even vote Tory
Though he knew they had the breeding
And wealth that could help you, and though
The local candidate's daughter
Had by chance the same name as me.

Yet at sixty-three he went out
One evening, furtive after dark
But swashbuckling, down to the polls

To vote for a man who once worked
On the railways; a guard, Father thought.

THE POSTILION HAS BEEN STRUCK BY LIGHTNING

He was the best postilion
I ever had. That summer in Europe
Came and went
In striding thunder-rain.
His tasselled shoulders bore up
More bad days than he could count
Till he entered his last storm in the mountains.

You to whom a postilion
Means only a cocked hat in a museum
Or a light
Anecdote, pity this one
Burnt at milord's expense far from home
Having seen every sight
But never anyone struck by lightning.

FOUR YEARS AFTER

'The perfectly preserved body of a British mountaineer was found near Courmayeur yesterday more than four years after he fell to his death on the Géant glacier.'

Yes, this was my husband, I
Cannot say 'is' though he has
Not changed since his dying day
Four years ago. Certainly
Ice is strong as saintliness
To keep corruption away.

I have altered in these years,
Better or less rightly wed,
Uglier or handsomer
Than I was then. All my tears
Rolled, grief like cargo shifted,
Grew and was cut like my hair.

I have moved but he not once,
For fifty moons not one cell.
Look at his glassy aplomb
Which has not been splintered since
Out of death and life he fell
To nothing. I could kill him.

A DREAM OF HANGING

He rang me up
In a dream,
My brother did.
He had been hanged
That morning,
Innocent,
And I had slept
Through the striking
Of the clock
While it had taken place,
Eight,
Just about time enough
For it to happen.
He spoke to me
On the telephone
That afternoon
To reassure me,
My dear brother
Who had killed nobody,
And I asked him,
Long distance,
What it had felt like
To be hanged.
'Oh, don't worry, lovey', he said,
'When your time comes.
It tickled rather.'

THE CHEMIST'S DREAM

When I started on my life's work
My early ambition was bold
To the point of naïveté.
It was to change things into gold,

To make meadows stiffer than corn
Twanging in the wind like a lyre,
To find rabbits in the last swath
Paralysed with gold not terror,

To make towns like missals painted
By lavish monks, a stiff-necked swan,
A gay witch melting in the fire,
Spinning tops brighter than Saturn.

Subtler I next looked for long life,
The elixir of never-die.
The tetchiness of old people
And their hairbreadth sleep bothered me.

I wanted to keep them clever,
To be relied on. I included
Myself in this discovery
But once again was evaded.

For I am poor and past my prime
And now the third part of my quest
Needles me, to find the liquid
That teachers call the alkahest.

It will dissolve everything
It comes in contact with, the noose,
The throne, lutes and battering rams,
It is power, easy to use.

It will create no such problems
As wealth and eternal life set,
Except one, what to keep it in.
Which I will solve when I find it.

YOUNG WIDOW

It is a luxury at my age
To say 'I am too old' when asked to marry.
Autumn leaves, fading coals and sunset
Are metaphors to state that I am weary

But no more than that; sunset does not
Become darkness, nor a live coal a dead one.
Perhaps I should have called in the stars
And proved that no one born under Scorpion

Can take up with a Crab. Class or race
Might have been good excuses, or heart scared
By sorrow. It is deft and polite to tell lies
To a suitor. The truth is, I am dead tired.

On Saturday evening I said no,
But on Sunday morning walked in bad weather,
My own mistress, around the churchyard
Where people older than I lay together.

CHRISTMAS EVE

The roofs over the shops
Are grey and quiet already.
In two hours from now
Light and noise will drain
From counter and cash desk
Into the streets and away.

People will go home
To windows that all year
Turned into their rooms
But goggle outwards now
With lit-up trees.

Tinsel wriggles in the heating.
Everything hangs.

As it gets dark a drunk
Comes tacking up the road
In a white macintosh
Charming as a yacht.

PICTURE OF WORKERS RESTING

You lie cooling and sleeping, the heat
Just round the corner of the haystack
And the work spread out over the field.

Your two billhooks put tidily down
And each pair of shoes taken off look
Much more like a couple than you do

Though man and wife you lie side by side
Apparently trusting each other.
Rest from work seems no real bond at all.

How very old-fashioned it all is.
The cart now stands in a museum
Of ancient crafts, the clothes have rotted.

A Marxist critic says the painter
Understood perfectly your bowed heads
And degradation. Perhaps he did,

But more profoundly, as creator
Not critic, saw his own flesh and blood
Lying there and did not ask himself

If you would have been quick at learning
To read, given the chance, or worthy
Landowners, given a piece of land.

WITCH

I shall see justice done.
I shall protect time
From monkish, cowardly men
Who say this life is not all
And do not respect the clock.

On those who will not escape
I shall see justice done.
I have courage to use
Wax and the killing pin
On behalf of prisoners.

I cut off the pilot's thumb
Because his compass failed.
I shall see justice done
Whenever the homeward bound
Mistake their true home.

In my black pointed heart
I cherish the good of all.
With storms, potions and blood
I shall see justice done
For I know goodness well.

Never shall bogus love –
Habit, duty or weakness –
Win any mercy from me.
By the light of my long burning
I shall see justice done.

LOVE SONG

Never be fool enough to think
The wrecking sea will cast up
Anything worth the salvaging,
A gold plate or a cup,
Silk or a piece of furniture,
Any vestige you can save,
Now your cargo, shining like a fish,
Is baled up in a wave.

Neither believe there is only shore,
That you can stamp your foot
And shut the door in the cliff side
To keep the ocean out,
For you cannot stop the sea mist
From fingering things, nor rub
The seagulls from your tumbling sky
Now land is at an ebb.

Let them swallow each other, soil
And water, and fish and bait.
In vertigo lies your only hope
For if you can admit
No difference between sea and land
You may find your love again,
Changed but with greater scope,
Re-born an amphibian.

THE TALE

The tale was always simple – once
A beautiful princess
Slept past the seasons and a prince
Brought time back in a kiss.

When sun and shadow flung the tweed
Of April on the wall,
Gay as a bobbin she wound up
The light along the hall

As she walked by. And yet she slept
Under the summer, till
The golden corn stepped down from day
And harvest had its will,

Until the prince obeyed a map
He could not understand,
Until his horse ran like a flame
Across the windy land.

Oh, magic is as hard to scan
As a skylark. Every cause,
Every effect is a single moon
Lit from enchanting laws.

Until the spinning of the kiss
No minstrel could have told
How rich the prince rode in from life
Across the dying gold,

And the far land where such a tale
Was reasonable, has made
Our falling leaves and rising suns
Enchanted and afraid.

Arthur J. Bull

Author's Introduction

I began to write under the influence of the Age of magnificence, of hyperbole – the Elizabethan.

Everything must be superlative – a thousand kisses, a million something else. There are traces of this in 'The Wind' (strongest force), in 'Samarkand' (most remote and splendid city), in 'The Windmill', again power and drive. (Did not Longfellow begin his poem, 'Behold, a giant am I'!)

But Shakespeare himself reacted, and wrote, 'My mistress' eyes are nothing like the sun . . .' The magnificent must yield to the average, youth to maturity and the unreal to the real.

And as reality dawns we see new aspects, new conflicts. In 'Sargon', which still has a strong touch of the hyperbolic (the 'greatest' monarch), a new theme appears, the conflict between two Faiths.

But there is another vital conflict, that between Man and Nature. Too much, and we are beaten, submerged, by the scrub, the weeds, the jungle ('Nature'). Too little, and we die of starvation in the desert, in the waste. (In two sonnets, not printed here, I have tried to express this pressure of the great deserts of Asia on the green oases. And yet the desert is also a refuge from the clutter of 'civilization' – 'I am Drawn Still to the Desert'.)

Furthermore, man creates problems for himself: perhaps he makes a 'civilization' which is bound to run down, to break up ('Modernismus'). Even when he builds a new temple he is not sure whether it is a cathedral or a railway station. Contrast my other sonnet (not included here), 'The Cathedral', where the genuine mediaeval building is called 'stupendous work of credal man'! But man is losing his creeds. The bureaucrat throws his deadening net ever closer to stifle all individual activity, and even God Himself is turned like the bureaucrat's wooden gate into a little wooden image to be set on a shelf. Religion becomes a mere matter of social custom ('His Theology').

Meanwhile the battle of life goes on incessantly. We rove and search for happiness, or just for a living, but in the end Time will strike us down ('The Enemies'). And when War actually rages, many a decent man catches a packet, while rogues and high-ups do themselves well in the safety of the rear ('This and That').

There are many more things I could say, but I will end on a little more comforting note if I can.

Whatever our troubles, however black the future, there are always moments of satisfaction, even of joy. The sight of a gloriously blossoming tree ('Richness'), or an early Spring-tide hour ('February Thaw'), or even the simplest things of all, just the rain-puddles in the lane ('November'), may bring their own balances against the weight of the world's woe. And 'The Acorn' always holds promise for the future.

NATURE

Do not be taken in
By grace of water, smile of sky:
We are beleaguered garrison,
And it is time we buy.

Our foes are myriadminded—
Bees like dragons hum,
Wasps are tigers of the air,
Spider sits plotting in her lair
How to achieve a general doom,
Weave in one universal web
Our cities proud and palaces.

Seas wash our bones from kindly air
Into the deep thalassic cave,
And every upland tarn extends a fair
Smooth invitation to the grave;
Under the shining water lies
A house from which no bride may rise.

Nature's the ancient enemy
No man of war can put to flight,
And that dark line of green you see
Is creeping on you in the night:
No-one may contract out of this
Embrace and marriage of the abyss.

THE WIND

After these long still days of frost and fire,
The sun destructive glowing his desire,
After the ringing iron on the road,
The January sky's impending load,
After the snow impertinently thrown
On rich and poor; the long surcease of noise,
Then, broken by the running streams alone,
A meretricious thaw, that troubles boys—
After all this, it is not ill to wake,

And hear the redskin wind about the stake,
Howling, and from your bedroom eyrie know,
World-currents have, so late, begun to blow:
That, cradled in the parish, you can share
An ocean-travelling, unmastered air;
That you can range, and O, rejoice with it
Beyond the grasp of iron winter's wit!

Wind is the present, and regrets no past,
Tears down the rigid house of winter's waste;
Wind in the metaphysic of the sky,
Omnipotently puts negation by:
I hear its call, Come out and celebrate
The living year. Wind opens winter's gate.
I hear it raging in the pines, and see
The poplar bend, that vext, that female tree;
I hear it, knowing in the dawn of day,
This turmoil comes a long Atlantic way.
It is importunate, and takes no keep,
Of watching misery, or windowed sleep;
Lets our close-printed page of passion be,
Offers no commentary; wind is free.
And yet with giant hand it breaks the bar,
That held me in, and lets me travel far:
Out of this day, and yesterday, I go,
Into the fairest region time can show,
And, for this moment, absolutely live,
In what will never be, time's fugitive.

THE WINDMILL

High, over the fen,
Fixed, in the rushing air,
A windmill, there,
Modelled and made by men.

Silent the plain lies,
Meek under load,
Heavy with harvest, the road
Ribbons, the crow flies:

COLBERT

And over the plain high,
Fierce as a dragon, fire
In the heart of the fen, and desire,
Draws, devours the rye;

Draws and devours the wheat,
Relishes, rich, the corn,
Where lonely, sharp in scorn,
He calls for the tribute set.

His anger fierce on the fen,
His rage high over the wheat,
The taste of his triumph sweet,
As he spoils the season again.

He points a finger high,
To the mathematic sky,
Calls to the rush and the rain,
To the gale, he may grind again.

And stark as the finger of God,
He lays upon the line,
Of tilth and term, the load
Of purpose, of design.

RICHNESS

There is speed and stress and richness here for the eye,
Beauty everywhere, bold and strongly striding,
Clouds tumbling, teeming, in trouble of sky,
Hugely wind-herded, riding and over-riding:
White in the West, mainward, the galleons rising,
With pressure, constancy, and pride of sailing,
Breasted, abounding, will stay for no man's hailing,
Wind-colts, wanton in this their exercising.

So welkin-world waxes, and as the skies
Cumber, discumber, green grass-glory lies,
Ravin'd about one, rolling, a sunlight, a sea,
Wave in the wind-rush silken – and, light as love,
A glitter of lantern-leaves is gold above,
Gathering spread sky-scurry all to one tree!

THE ACORN

This is the seed of scorn; prolific swine
Munch it with beechmast in the heathen wild;
Far from the habitations built of men
It lies, a giant's lost, neglected child.

Unseen among the many, it is one,
A small perfection in the sandy waste;
And fashions, working in itself alone,
A form, that does not know the pulse of haste.

There, springing in the suns of yesterday,
Triumphant under chastisement of rain,
And reaching to the winters that shall be
It draws the profit of that long delay,
Joins the ill-parted centuries again,
And lives once more in the great timeless tree.

FEBRUARY THAW

There's comfort in black February firs,
Against a streaky sky; no longer show,
As yesterday, the unforgiving snow,
The icicle, and meditative stirs
A little wind, that scarcely knows its way,
Having, between the rib and rock, come far,
Seeing no tenderness, familiar,
In all the field of January's war.

O February's infantry is light,
Deploys, at once victoriously takes
Possession of each vantage knoll, each tree –
Bright February, laked on every lea,
Ripples in mischief, excellently makes
Mock of old Winter, storm and coming night!

NOVEMBER

I hear them say, There has been too much of rain!
And, seeing the gift spread shining from the sky,
I am happy, puddle-pleased, and know not why,

As if I held the dry in great disdain:
And again, hearing the plodders and ploughmen plain,
I catch at the cowheel cups with greedy eye,
Whose fallen innocence is one with the sky,
Whose ignorance delays the winter grain:
Their shallow spill and overflow is more
To me, their brief unhappy fleeting day,
Their modesty, than some Atlantic pride,
Thundering on a catastrophic shore;
'The ground is waterlogged!' – Ah, let them say –
I would not change these shoals for ocean's tide.

I AM DRAWN STILL TO THE DESERT

I am drawn still to the desert, and cannot go –
I am weary of this, the intersected land,
The straying hedges fidget me, and the unplanned
Straggle of yesterday, the untidy crow,
Perpetual parish: O I am sick of the show.

There is too much here that is rooted, too much old,
And the green is no more gracious in my sight;
I dream of an emptiness, a bare delight,
A dry monotony of sanded gold,
Where the wind-clean bone is eloquently white.

And walking the lane alone I see the trees,
The cabins, and gates, a litter in my way,
Coming between me, and what I would say,
A screen, a trouble, to me, even while they please,
And I would slice the skyline like a cheese.

There must be comfort in the desert's face:
No stack or stave or stick to vex the eye,
No salutation, friend or passerby,
No print of trafficking, no crossing-place –
And in that vacancy, a wind of grace!

ON THE FEN: A STORMY DAY NEAR HECKINGTON

Persepolis is great with pomp and pride,
High kings through Babylon in triumph ride;
The net of Tyre is cast about the sea,
And Rome sends roots through Europe like a tree –
But there is greatness too in little things
That can rebuke the valiancy of kings,
And I would come a thousand miles again
To see roofs riding on the storm-struck fen,
Cottages more courageous to my sight,
Than great ships going down into the night.

SARGON

How I should like to see great Babylon –
Tiglath-Pileser walking on the wall,
Sargon above his captives giant-tall,
And the great bulls triumphant in their stone:
Not ancient images, but paint-new, clear,
Hard, bright, and modern, when the City rose
Colossal out of clay against her foes,
Filling the desert with a word of fear.

There, before Charlemain or Mahomet,
Great Caesar, or the Lord of Macedon,
Ere the first brick of village Rome was set,
See Nabonassar with his iron rod, –
Or, carved and silent on the very stone,
Nimrod, the great antagonist of God.

THE ENEMIES

I hew and hack at Space, at lands and seas,
Cut cantles here, and lop a league off there,
Play Alexander, conquer by degrees
Sprawling old Earth, who used to domineer
So much upon our infancy, when we
Looked fearfully from pale and narrow pen
Upon a field as wide as any sea,
The unknown kingdom of tall stamping men.

Now, when it pleases me, I take my way,
Leap Channel like a brook, and stride or ride
Upon the carpet stretches to Cathay,
Pressing back boundaries on every side:

But while I march, a king, o'er land and sea,
Time comes behind, and says, 'I follow thee!'

THIS AND THAT

How they enjoyed themselves the military gentlemen,
writing history in terms of boots and blood,
tracing the course of armies through moor and fen,
trotting hussars, sloggers whose feet were not so good.

Columns wind through long campaigns and their coats are red,
officers gallop and curse and wine and make some love;
in the chancelleries the last word is never said,
and pickets take potshots at (Heavens!) the heavenly dove.

But in the grind of guns, the cannons' racket,
stealthier sounds are lost – the swing of scythe,
except one Scythe when a pal has caught a packet;
and the husbandman mows long to pay his tithe.

HIS THEOLOGY

(*With apologies to Walt Whitman*)

I measured god from side to side,
he's three feet long and two feet wide;
he has no head, for how could he
use brains, to make the world we see?
He has no feet to wander round
and see such litter on the ground;
he has no heart-beats warm and loud,
no ears to hear the praying crowd:
taking him altogether, I
do not think much of deity.

For this the Romans at the stake
would burn me if they could,
methodists drown me in a lake,
and baptists spill my blood;
Jehovah's Witnesses would gnash
their yellow teeth and use the lash;
only the cheery Anglican
would say, 'You're part of His great plan',
and ask me in to see the Choir –
'A bit of Norman work you know, and so's the Squire!'

COLLECTOR'S NOTE

I bought God in an antique shop,
Carved from a curious ebony:
I thought he would not want to stop
Where there was little life to see.

With careful hand one reached him down,
And wrapped him up in paper brown;
He did not say a word, poor god,
Although he must have found it odd.

I took him home, and put him safe
Upon a shelf, where he could see
Just opposite, the busy cafe,
And all those going in for tea.

I have not asked him yet if he
Wants to go back to heaven high,
Take his old job again, and be
Arbiter of our destiny.

He does not seem to care, I find
For trouble, or amusement now,
It does not seem to cross his mind
That there are planets past the Plough.

So he sits there in wooden state,
And smiles as if he had a date
With some remote eternity,
When nothing will exist, but He.

STUDY IN PUNCTUATION

They began to build a church, stone and brick,
and lay pieces heavy, solid, in the clay, ground,
making the wall straight, the base thick,
and deep down too, buried, was hid the Faith, profound.

But a strange thing happened: as the box rose
wherein they would prison their god, and enclose
his favour for all time, to their children's children, and more,
the Faith died – and as the coping-stone fell into place,
one, wiser than the rest, looked up, and saw No-god's face
smiling at them from the rim of the sky
before he took wing for a long journey; perhaps he will
return,
by and by.

QUATRAIN

A strictly mathematic God
draws out the Universe with rule and line:
means well no doubt – but I am bloody odd,
and cannot fit myself to His design.

SEVERITY

In this age we must seek the Byzantine,
Remote, unfeeling, geometric Gods,
Man with his mush-world savagely at odds,
Fierce in the hard unyielding sculptor's line.

Long must we stare and wonder at the plain
Precision of mosaic, and in that,
See cosmos tessellated in the flat,
The sacred square establishéd again.

Order must come: for surely we are sick,
Seeing rococo writhe about the dome,
And the full fleshy deities of Rome
Plastered upon the altar-pieces thick.

Is Man the measure? – We abominate
His carnal error, curve and trunk and limb;
Our fallen idol: and we loathe in him
The crawling plump persistent larval state.

Whatever God is, He at least is not
This pound of sausage stuffed into a skin:
Away with the anthropomorphic sin,
Let all the Adam-seed be unbegot!

That when the vulgar come to see their God,
Pure, mathematical, severe, and high,
He may be figured, abstract as the sky,
To strike their softness with an iron rod:

And as they whisper, giggle, at His feet,
May the great peace and majesty of Mind,
Into their littleness some entry find,
And set at last a term to their conceit,

That they may feel, before it is too late,
The folly they have ageless wallowed in,
Their need, that cries aloud for discipline,
And, terrible, the straitness of the gate.

THE NEW COVENTRY CATHEDRAL

The last century took its courage in both hands
And built a Railway Station,
In iron, good Gothic to wit,
Like a Cathedral; great was the consternation.

Now this age has shown its guts, its grit,
By designing a Cathedral like a
Railway Station.
O glorious revolution of history,
O gratifying revenges of grinning Time!

The steam engine whistles and puffs through
the gloomy aisles of St. Pancras,
While the voice of the Bishop calls thin
But clear,
Across the tracks, clerical and severe,

Where bewildered and would-be passengers
Stray, looking for the train to bliss they
Feel should be theirs.
O tempora, O mores!
All change please: tickets ready;
Hassocks may be hired for the journey, and tea
If you wish; the kindly guard will take
A cup with the canons, and a stray missionary.
We know where we're going,
But we don't know when we'll get there.
Take your seats please;
The sidesmen will tuck you in and close the doors,
All aboard for the heavenly floors;
Steam is up, the din is terriffic, and many
Cannot find a seat:
In the steam and the heat
Heaven is forgotten, our destination,
And we almost think it a Church, not a Station.

MODERNISMUS: or, PRAYER FOR STANDSTILL

Nobody may grow old now, grandfathers are out;
times change and we must damn well change with them;
no ripening, old wine, in the cellars of time,
maturing into wisdom, gathering honey and gall,
respectfully heard by the sons and the grandsons,
crowning a patriarchal age with words of heeded counsel:
there is no long age any more, the reigns and the
consulships come and go swift as days and nights,
the abysses gape, the razorbridge holds, we tread
to the farther side breathless and daily shaken,
helped by younger hands, and younger pitying unpitying heads;
fashions flutter and fly, strange inventions
roar in the factories over the garden paling,
the very facts betray us, and the thinkers
continually bring up new proofs, new theories,
two years back is out of date and twenty prehistoric,
before you can turn round the boy next door
has grown up and gone to the wars, and the girl
wearing blue jeans in a munition factory;
your half-completed life is already sliced into
four or five strata, and you await those to come
helpless, drifting on the lee shore of the future,

praying only wreck may not be total, something,
life, a barrow of goods, if not honour, may be
saved from ineluctable disaster.
How fortunate
those white-bearded jelly-bellies who prosed
and prognosticated in the days before progress,
when the Great White Queen ruled the ignorant
black men, and cigarettes were not yet the pillars
of the tottering State! O Lord, take us back to
that primal innocence – the Garden of Even,
before the odd became so very very Odd, and the
current began to set so unmistakably towards
the cataract whose sound is always in our ears:
Let us for Christ's sake continue in one
stay, petrify us with thy grace,
stand still you ever-rolling spheres of heaven,
maintain and keep thy fearful servants Lord,
O keep us, in our place!

TASTES

I like a blonde who wears a silver fox,
And nothing else, above her bobbysox;
I like a tree that stands as great as Jove,
On guard above the mortals who make love.
I like the crankshaft of a huge machine,
Superbly turning, metal-bright and clean;
I like the little birds that come to fight
And quarrel for a crust, when snow is white.
I like the scholar's mind, that cuts as deep
As any surgeon, through time's rubbish heap;
I like the little boy, who does not think
His work complete, without a smear of ink.
I like the lion-frieze on Sargon's wall,
The strong three-quarter running with the ball,
The chequered pattern dancing light and free,
Where sun and wind make love to one fair tree,
And on the stage before me always set,
Many more groupings choice and delicate,
But most of all, I think, Patricia's hair,
Just now, is all that's excellent and rare –
Burnished, and smooth, and with a ribbon red,
Charmingly tied upon her empty head.

DEINOSAURS

I love the Deinosaurs, their padded bulk,
Their little heads, so clearly made to sulk,
Their decorative ridges, and each plate
Of armour, so fantastic, big and blate
I like its overlapping – how they must
Have lumbered, moving under all that crust,
Immortal pies, and nourished, if they could,
Those craving guts, so long before the Flood.

I like the Brontosaurus, with his tail
Busy among the saplings like a flail,
His long long back, his hundred feet of span,
So much more satisfying than mere man.
How long it must have taken for a pin
Stuck in his tail, to send its message in!
I like his jointed neck that could uprear
Some forty feet, and round the parish peer,
A useful friend to have, a sentinel,
A mower, roller, for the lawn as well,
A gentle creature, like a donkey or
A camel – such a harmless deinosaur.

I like the Stegosaurus even now,
Though one would scarcely harness *him* to plough:
He had his points – at least life was not dull,
When he was prowling for his bellyfull.
They must, in their own heavyfooted way,
Have made the most of their Jurassic day;
Even their loves, had one been there to see,
Would have made conversation over tea;
I should have beat it when Triceratops
And loving partner, had their Combined Ops.,
And two Tyrannosauri would have made
A pretty havoc in some bowery glade!

THE BUREAUCRAT

He gets himself, after a long campaign,
with grief and setback and pain,
a larger carpet, a bigger and better chair,
a desk to make colleagues stare:

so in triumph seated he plans to throw
his empire far and wide,
he would be pasha, sultan, nay even more –
by proper protocol
eventually deified,
reign GOD, from shore to farthest shore,
over a vast-extending sea
of ever-thicker carpet floor
ruling divinely you and me.

With what beneficence,
and nod divine,
his goodness will upon the Public shine,
until two careful coves come in one day,
to take the Lord our God away.

SAMARKAND

Alas, I shall not shuffle in the sand
Of Barbary, or play my trombone, woe
Is me, in any place but Pimlico,
And I must pine in Putney's pleasant land:
My life and lines are resolutely planned,
Blue-printed, and rebellion is no go;
Besides, each Empire has the same old show,
And there are petrol pumps in Samarkand.

There is one place I'd visit – it is far
Far back, beyond the torn-off Calendar,
A thousand days and nights – and there is none,
Can turn the key of time, and let me pass
Where grew astonishing that withered grass,
None show me now the shining of that sun.

THE JUNGLE

The jungle is about me: I am content,
Not fearing now the lion, or the snake,
Nor even the darkness; and what was to me,
Wan from the white-world, shadowy descent,
Deep into shunned, unsunned, ill-lying lake,
Proves friendly, gracious, full of piety:

Each trodden path is old; the jungle way
I wisely pace, is not of yesterday;
In these bare customary paths I find
A pensive shade, an uncomplaining grief,
Firm as the baobab, that sacred tree;
And in the maze is music to my mind,
A silent, involuted, mute relief,
Old as the sky, more settled than the sea.

D. J. Enright

Author's Introduction

Apart from 'Along the River' and the nine pieces (the first in this selection) from *The Terrible Shears* (a sequence concerned with growing up in the English Midlands in the 1920's and 30's), all the poems printed here were written in and about foreign countries – though naturally I hope their interest is not too severely restricted by that fact. Japan, Thailand, South-East Asia, Germany – I lived there, not as a visitor, but as a working resident. These poems have to do with public events rather than private (the distinction holds up to a point): war and the aftermath of war, afflictions arising out of race and nationality, the co-presence of obvious poverty and conspicuous consumption (as remarked on in a fairly light-hearted Christmas spirit in 'Means Test'), specific political situations as they affect not the top brass but the 'common' – usually unpolitical – 'man'. The song in 'Streets' was a real song, and its real composer realized at the last moment that it would be prudent to change its location from 'Hanoi' to 'Saigon'. The children in 'Children Killed in War' were real children, though whether South Vietnamese or North Vietnamese I cannot now remember.

That the poems relate or comment on actual incidents does not of course make them good poems, any more than press reports necessarily qualify as artistic objects. 'Truth' and 'sincerity' may be necessary to poetry, but in poetry they are factors much more complex than their names suggest. But whether or not the poems have any literary value (and that is what poems ought to aim at), I still like to think that just possibly they may justify themselves as truthful memorials of the small events which so easily get lost to sight in the large movements of history.

From *The Terrible Shears*

TWO BAD THINGS IN INFANT SCHOOL

Learning bad grammar, then getting blamed for it:
Learning Our Father which art in Heaven.

Bowing our heads to a hurried nurse, and
Hearing the nits rattle down on the paper.

AND TWO GOOD THINGS

Listening to Miss Anthony, our lovely Miss,
Charming us dumb with *The Wind in the Willows*.

Dancing Sellinger's Round, and dancing and
Dancing it, and getting it perfect forever.

TRAINING

How docile we were, how orderly! Empire Day,
Armistice Day, and all that religious instruction!
They were training us to die for something –
It meant nothing, only holidays and queer emotions.

Forty years later, walking in Canton, I encounter
A mass of orderly children – they are listening
Intently, with every sign of agreement,
To a horror story about red-haired imperialists.

I slope past fearfully. But to them I'm no more
Than a comical flower in this well-kept park.
Keeping one's eyes on teacher is far more important.
As yet they haven't learnt to connect.

SUNDAY

My mother's strongest religious feeling
Was that Catholics were a sinister lot;
She would hardly trust even a lapsed one.
My father was a lapsed Catholic.

Yet we were sent to Sunday school.
Perhaps in the spirit that others
Were sent to public schools. It
Might come in useful later on.

In Sunday school a sickly adult
Taught the teachings of a sickly lamb
To a gathering of sickly children.

It was a far cry from that brisk person
Who created the heaven and the earth in
Six days and then took Sunday off.

The churches were run by a picked crew
Of bad actors radiating insincerity.
Not that one thought of them in that way,
One merely disliked the sound of their voices.
I cannot recall one elevated moment in church,
Though as a choirboy I pulled in a useful
Sixpence per month.

Strange, that a sense of religion should
Somehow survive all this grim buffoonery!
Perhaps that brisk old person does exist,
And we are living through his Sunday.

SPOILT

How well we were catered for!
No wonder we lost our teeth.
Chewy locust, thick strong liquorice sticks,
Aniseed balls, bull's eyes, and sherbet . . .

Later in my prime, at elegant parties in the
Orient (but where was the sherbet? Where
The locust?), I met caviare and smoked salmon
And various oriental delicacies.

They were no sort of substitute.
But happily I found a new strong taste,
Easy on the teeth too,
Whisky, gin, brandy and ginger.

INSURANCE

One spot of cheer in the Midlands gloom
Was our Dublin uncle
Who sent us shamrock each St Patrick's Day
And ebullient letters
On paper headed THE PHOENIX ASSURANCE COMPANY LTD.
He was the family success
(His photograph looks like Mickey Rooney
He could sign his name in careful Gaelic)
He moved in the corridors of power.

He came across for his brother's funeral
Pensively noting the widow and orphans at the graveside.
Something had to be said about our insurance.

He had borrowed, he intimated, the company's notepaper.
Faith, he worked there, he was a janitor there
He moved in the corridors.

Romantic Ireland was dead and gone.

ALWAYS LEARNING

The gym teacher was big, handsome and
Dashing. He pronounced *tooth* as *tuth*
And *food* as *fud*, which much intrigued us.
He talked of rugger like a lover,
And rode a motorbike, big, handsome
And dashing, which we much admired.

He broke a leg in an accident
On his bike, and couldn't perform
The exercises he required of us:
He described them in words, like an elegy,
A lovely man! We groaned twice over,
For ourselves, and our disabled hero.

The months went by, he ceased to limp, but
In the gym was still the thwarted cripple.
We groaned for our sweating selves alone.

Do as I say, not as I do:
We had gained in worldly wisdom,
We had lost an admiration.

UGLY NECK

There seems to be a large gap
Somewhere about here.
If repression is at work
Then repression works efficiently,
In this sphere.

I don't remember learning about sex
In the school lavatories;
Though I remember the lavatories.

With a great effort I call up
Certain goings-on in the rear rows
Of the Physics class. I can't believe it.
That Welsh master was so sharp
You couldn't blow your nose
Without him glaring.

At one time or another
Some slightly special one or other –
But to kiss a girl
Would have seemed like criminal assault.
There was one called Pearl
Who would quote bits from Rosalind
In *As You Like It*, leaving me confused.
Once at a party I stepped heavily
On her hand, and was appalled.
In a strange way she seemed to like it.
I was glad to go home and study *The Prelude*.

It was homework and rugger; then
It was essays and walks to Grantchester.
Perhaps we were great Platonic lovers then.
Perhaps there is nothing to remember.

LARGE MERCIES

I remember the schoolgirl under the bus,
Her bicycle lying in her blood,
And the driver in tears, saying over
And over, 'I'll never drive again.'

I remember too, her leg was amputated,
And when she passed her exams
The local paper announced it proudly,
And again when she married.

That means it wasn't a bad life.
No one was dragged out of bed by
Armed men. Children weren't speared
Or their brains dashed out. I don't
Remember seeing a man starve to death.

That's something we shouldn't forget –
That we don't remember things like that.

* * *

WARM PROTEST

To shoot a man against the National Library wall!
– The East unsheathes its barbarous finger-nail.

In Europe this was done in railway trucks,
Cellars underground, and such sequestered nooks.

To wound a Library wall with bullet nicks!
Really hardly cultured. No respect for books.

How shall I ever (never easy, as you know)
Persuade the boys and girls to use the Library now?

I – I assure you – speak but as a teacher –
Lover of learning – in no way any traitor –

Good God! – don't think that I've an axe to grind –
It's only – it was simply – merely – never mind.

THE HARD CORE

You can find them anywhere.
In better managed states, you'll have to look:
They're there, unadvertised behind the hoardings,
In casual self-concealing tenements,
Asleep by public fountains.
In badly managed states, they walk the streets
Free citizens, free to beg.
        One is a junkie. Another armless.
One is spoiled by rheumatism (from working
Long hours on bridges or public fountains).
Some were born too weak to keep their strength up.
The commoner suffer merely from consumption,
And dysentery, and child-bearing, and anaemia.
Nothing, it seems, can dissolve this hard core
Of disorder and disease.
    The anarchist moves among them delicately
(Despite his age), with cast-off bread and
Clothing, small change and opium dottles,
Little gifts for his admirers
(As they would be, if they knew, if they'd had
The chance to know). They prove his point,
Without once opening their surly mouths.
They are the only people who count.
        He counts them.
Sometimes wondering, as he washes his hands
At a public fountain: Is he sorry?
Is he an anarchist because he is sorry?
Is he sorry because he's an anarchist?
Grateful, at last, when one of them spits
In his face. Breaking a law.

AM STEINPLATZ

Benches round a square of grass.
You enter by the stone that asks,
    'Remember those whom Hitlerism killed'.
'Remember those whom Stalinism killed',
Requests the stone by which you leave.

This day, as every other day,
I shuffle through the little park,
    from stone to stone,
From conscience-cancelling stone to stone,
Peering at the fading ribbons on the faded wreaths.

At least the benches bear their load,
Of people reading papers, eating ices,
Watching aeroplanes and flowers,
Sleeping, smoking, counting, cuddling.
    Everything but heed those stony words.
They have forgotten. As they must.
Remember those who live. Yes, they are right.
    They must.

A dog jumps on the bench beside me.
Nice doggie: never killed a single Jew, or Gentile.
Then it jumps on me. Its paws are muddy, muzzle wet.
Gently I push it off. It likes this game of war.

At last a neat stout lady on a nearby bench
Calls tenderly, 'Komm, Liebchen, komm!
Der Herr' – this public-park-frau barks –
    'does not like dogs!'

Shocked papers rustle to the ground;
Ices drip away forgotten; sleepers wake;
The lovers mobilize their distant eyes.
    The air strikes cold.
There's no room for a third stone here.
    I leave.

NO OFFENCE

In no country
Are the disposal services more efficient.

Standardized dustbins
Fit precisely into the mouth of a large cylinder
Slung on a six-wheeled chassis.
Even the dustbin lid is raised mechanically
At the very last moment.
You could dispose of a corpse like this
Without giving the least offence.

In no country
Are the public lavatories more immaculately kept.
As neat as new pins, smelling of pine forests,
With a roar like distant Wagner
Your sins are washed away.

In no country
Do the ambulances arrive more promptly.
You are lying on the stretcher
Before the police, the driver, the bystanders and the
neighbouring shopkeepers
Have finished lecturing you.

In no country
Are the burial facilities more foolproof.
A few pfennigs a week, according to age,
Will procure you a very decent funeral.
You merely sign on the dotted line
And keep your payments regular.

In no country
Are the disposal services more efficient
– I reflect –
As I am sorted out, dressed down, lined up,
Shepherded through the door,
Marshalled across the smooth-faced asphalt,
And fed into the mouth of a large cylinder
Labelled 'Lufthansa'.

THE MONUMENTS OF HIROSHIMA

The roughly estimated ones, who do not sort well
with our common phrases,
Who are by no means eating roots of dandelion,
or pushing up the daisies.

The more or less anonymous, to whom no human idiom
can apply,
Who neither passed away, or on,
nor went before, nor vanished on a sigh.

Little of peace for them to rest in, less of them
to rest in peace:
Dust to dust a swift transition, ashes to ash
with awful ease.

Their only monument will be of others' casting –
A Tower of Peace, a Hall of Peace, a Bridge of Peace
– who might have wished for something lasting,
Like a wooden box.

STREETS

The poem was entitled 'The Streets of Hanoi',
It told of falling bombs and death and destruction
And misery and pain and wastage.
The poem was set to music, which told of death
And destruction and misery and pain and wastage.

A hall was found to play it in, a singer to sing it,
An orchestra to accompany the singer, and a printer
To print the programme . . . Whereupon it was felt
(Things being what they happened to be) that
The song had better be called 'The Streets of Saigon'.

It was well sung, well played, and well received.

Truly poetry is international, just like music,
And falling bombs and death and destruction
And misery and pain and wastage,

Truly we only need one poet in the world
Since local references can be inserted by editors,
Theatre managers or clerks in the Culture Ministries.

CHILDREN KILLED IN WAR

A still day here,
Trees standing like a lantern show,
Cicadas, those sparse eaters, at their song,
The eye of silence, lost in soundlessness.

And then, no warning given,
Or if foreseen, then not to be escaped,
A well-aimed wind explodes,
And limbs of trees, which cannot run away,
May only hide behind each other.

Grant their death came promptly there,
Who died too soon,
That pain of parting was not long,
Roots ready to let fall their leaves.

The wind burns out,
The trees, what's left, resume their stand,
The singers stilled, an iron comb
Wrenched roughly through their lives.

While you, your thinking blown off course,
Design some simple windless heaven
Of special treats and toys,
Like picnic snapshots,
Like a magic-lantern show.

TERMINAL

A small boy, four years
Or so of age,
And tired and confused,
In a noisy, crowded building,
His ears still hurting
From some mysterious ailment.
He trails behind his parents,
Tired too, if less confused.

Then the people all take sides,
Like in a game,
His father joins the Caucasian file,
His mother the Other.
Which team is his team?
He hears them talking,
His English father, Chinese mother,
And the man who owns the building.

Who rubs his head:
'There's this queue and there's that queue,
There isn't any third queue.
I don't know what to say!'

Neither does the little boy,
He is tired and confused.
In front of him the two queues stretch away,
There isn't any third queue.

PITCHFORK DEPARTMENT

It was patent in this ancient city, paradise of
Statuary, that pigeons lacked respect for greatness.
Lucky statesmen, innocent generals and forgiven thinkers,

Their iron breasts befouled, their noble brows
Turned grey, their swords and croziers rusted,
Manuscripts illuminated, padded shanks gone leprous.

Yet the children loved the pigeons, it pleased the
Taxpayers to be used as perches. They walked our streets,
Sometimes were run over, did not disdain our bread.

So the city fathers, as humane as is befitting
In this age of letters and elections, set out
Drugged fodder: 'Let the sleeping birds be stacked

With care in corporation vehicles, and conveyed to
Some remote and rural district. Let them there be laid
In appropriate positions in their proper places.'

They slept the weekend through, lost in a dream
Of the Hall of the Thirty Thousand Buddhas, or the day
When every civil servant shall be issued with a public statue.

On Tuesday afternoon, from under their umbrellas,
The city fathers watched the homing pigeons, assiduous,
unresenting,
Bowels gently stimulated, natural functions unaffected.

MEANS TEST

The top people
Receive lots of Christmas cards and large
A foot square, in purple and gold
The Ministers and the M.P.s
The senior servants in sensitive services
The importers and exporters and industrialists
The presidents of shipping lines
The chairmen of airlines
They receive cards at Christmas both large and many
From Embassies and High Commissions
Executives and industrialists
Presidents of shipping lines
Chairmen of airlines.

Exempli gratia, Japan Air Lines
Arrives in the form of a huge fan and
Carries an appropriate message in several languages
And the minimum of advertising and
A work of art thrown in.

Tools of the trade
The company pays.

In your father's house
They will require large mansions
In which to hang their Christmas cards.

The bottom people
Receive fewer and smaller Christmas cards
In one single language
A simple message, the price is sometimes
Marked on the back
They send fewer and smaller cards at Christmas
The bottom people pay for their Christmas cards
Out of their own pocket.

In your father's house
They will only require small mansions
In which to hang their Christmas cards
And
Since they are used to paying out of their own pocket
Your father can charge them rent.

THE SENSITIVE PHILANTHROPIST

If I give you money,
Give you baksheesh,
Will you stay away
Until next week?

Since money talks
We don't need to,
Neither you to me
Nor me to you.

If I give you money
Will you make sure
That the others keep away,
Without me giving more?

Will you promise
To put to flight
All your legless colleagues
By day and by night?

If I give you money
Will you agree
To hide your stump away,
Where I can't see?

Will you state in writing
That it was done on purpose
And doesn't really hurt,
The arms, the legs, the nose?

Can't I send a cheque
Regular each week
By registered letter
So we need never meet?

IN THE JUNGLE

The soldier ants, the red-eyed starlings,
Go about their chores. Domestic lizards
Perpetrate their stock atrocities.

A slow hawk sweeps the sky in careful circles.
A gorged bat twitches in its sleep.

He sits at his typewriter, in this jungle,
A little man of letters, wondering
Who'll take the next bite, who'll be bitten.
It may be only fifteen hundred words
On some new travel book: to him it always
Feels like his last will and testament.

ALONG THE RIVER

They had pulled her out of the river. She was dead,
Lying against the rhododendrons sewn with spider's thread.
An oldish woman, in a shabby dress, a straggling stocking,
A worn, despairing face. How could the old do such a thing?

Now forty years have passed. Again I recall that poor
Thing laid along the River Leam, and I look once more.

They have pulled her out of the river. She is dead,
Lying against the rhododendrons sewn with spider's thread.
A youngish woman, in a sodden dress, a straggling stocking,
A sad, appealing face. How can the young do such a thing?

Seamus Heaney

Author's Introduction

Feeling into Words or Digging and Divining

Extracts from a lecture delivered to the Royal Society of Literature in October 1974

To analyse the craft of putting feelings into words is, inevitably I think, to talk about poetry as divination, poetry as revelation of the self to the self, as the restoration of the culture to itself; poems as elements of continuity, with the aura and authenticity of archaeological finds, where the buried shard has an importance that is not obliterated by the buried city; poetry as a dig, a dig for finds that end up by being plants.

'Digging', in fact, was the name of the first poem I wrote where I thought my feelings had got into words, or to put it more accurately, where I thought my *feel* had got into words. This was the first place where I felt I had done more than make an arrangement of words: I felt that I had let down a shaft into real life. I didn't care who thought what about it: somehow, it had surprised me by coming out with a stance and an idea that I would stand over:

> 'The cold smell of potato mould, the squelch and slap
> Of soggy peat, the curt cuts of an edge
> Through living roots awaken in my head.
> But I've no spade to follow men like them.
>
> Between my finger and my thumb
> The squat pen rests.
> I'll dig with it.'

I wrote it down ten years ago; yet perhaps I should say that I dug it up, because I have come to realize that it was laid down in me years before that even.

* * *

I don't want to overload 'Digging' with too much significance, but it is interesting as an example of what we call 'finding a voice'. Finding a voice means that you can get your own feeling into your own words and that your words have the feel of you about them; and I believe that it may not even be a metaphor, for a poetic voice is probably very intimately connected with the poet's natural voice, the voice that he hears as the ideal speaker of the lines he is making up.

But how do you find this voice? In practice, you hear it coming from somebody else, you hear something in another writer's sounds that flows in through your ear and enters the echo-chamber of your head and delights your whole nervous system in such a way that your reaction will be, 'Ah, I wish I had said that, in that particular way.' This other writer, in fact, has spoken something essential to you, something you recognize instinctively as a true sounding of aspects of yourself and your experience. And your first steps as a writer will be to imitate, consciously or unconsciously, those sounds that flowed in, that in-fluence.

* * *

I think technique is different from craft. Craft is what you can learn from other verse. Craft is the skill of making. It can be deployed without reference to the feelings or the self. Technique involves not only a poet's way with words, his management of metre, rhythm and verbal texture; it involves also a definition of his stance towards life, a definition of his own reality. Technique is what turns, in Yeats's phrase, 'the bundle of accident and incoherence that sits down to breakfast' into 'an idea, something intended, complete'. And if I were asked for a figure who represents pure technique, I would say a water diviner. You can't learn the craft of dowsing or divining – it's a gift for being in touch with what is there, hidden and real, a gift for mediating between the latent resource and the community that wants it current or released. The diviner resembles the poet in his function of making contact with what lies hidden, and in his ability to make palpable what was sensed or raised. When I called my second book of poems *Door into the Dark* I intended to gesture towards the idea of poetry as a point of entry into the buried life of the feelings or as a point of exit for it. Words themselves are doors; Janus is to a certain extent their deity, looking back to a ramification of roots and associations and forward to a clarification of sense and meaning. So there are a number of poems that arise out of the almost unnameable energies that, for me, hovered over certain bits of language and landscape.

* * *

The best moments are those when your mind seems to implode and words and images rush of their own accord into the vortex. Which happened to me once when the line 'We have no prairies' drifted into my head at bedtime, and loosened a fall of images that constitute the poem 'Bogland' (page 69).

I had been vaguely wishing to write a poem about bogland, chiefly because it is a landscape that has a strange assuaging effect on me, one with associations reaching back into early childhood. We used to hear about bog-butter, butter kept fresh for a great number of years under the peat. Then when I was at school the skeleton of an elk had been taken out of a bog nearby and a few of our neighbours had got their photographs in the paper, peering out across the antlers. So I began to get an idea of bog as the memory of the landscape, or as a landscape that remembered everything that happened in and to it. In fact, if you go round the National Museum in Dublin, you will realize that a great proportion of the most cherished heritage of Ireland was 'found in a bog'. Moreover, since memory was the faculty that supplied me with the first quickening of my own poetry, I had a tentative need to make a congruence between memory and bogland and, for the want of a better word, our national consciousness. And it all released itself after 'We have no prairies . . .' – but we have bogs. At that time I had been reading about the frontier and the west as an important myth in the American consciousness, so I set up – or rather, laid down – the bog as an answering Irish myth. I wrote it quickly the next morning, having slept on my excitement, and revised it on the hoof, from line to line, as it came.

Again, as in the case of 'Digging', the seminal impulse had been unconscious. I believe what generated the poem about memory was something lying beneath the very floor of memory, something I only connected with the poem months after it was written, which was a warning that older people would give us about going into the bog. They were afraid we might fall into the pools in the old workings so they put it about (and we believed them) that *there was no bottom* in the bogholes. Little did they – or I – know that I would filch it for the last line of a poem.

ANAHORISH

My 'place of clear water',
the first hill in the world
where springs washed into
the shiny grass

and darkened cobbles
in the bed of the lane.
Anahorish, soft gradient
of consonant, vowel-meadow,

after-image of lamps
swung through the yards
on winter evenings.
With pails and barrows

those mound-dwellers
go waist-deep in mist
to break the light ice
at wells and dunghills.

WHINLANDS

All year round the whin
Can show a blossom or two
But it's in full bloom now.
As if the small yolk stain

From all the birds' eggs in
All the nests of the spring
Were spiked and hung
Everywhere on bushes to ripen.

Hills oxidize gold.
Above the smoulder of green shoot
And dross of dead thorns underfoot
The blossoms scald.

Put a match under
Whins, they go up of a sudden.
They make no flame in the sun
But a fierce heat tremor

Yet incineration like that
Only takes the thorn.
The tough sticks don't burn,
Remain like bone, charred horn.

Gilt, jaggy, springy, frilled
This stunted, dry richness
Persists on hills, near stone ditches,
Over flintbed and battlefield.

BLACKBERRY-PICKING

Late August, given heavy rain and sun
For a full week, the blackberries would ripen.
At first, just one, a glossy purple clot
Among others, red, green, hard as a knot.
You ate that first one and its flesh was sweet
Like thickened wine: summer's blood was in it
Leaving stains upon the tongue and lust for
Picking. Then red ones inked up and that hunger
Sent us out with milk-cans, pea-tins, jam-pots
Where briars scratched and wet grass bleached our boots.
Round hayfields, cornfields and potato-drills
We trekked and picked until the cans were full,
Until the tinkling bottom had been covered
With green ones, and on top big dark blobs burned
Like a plate of eyes. Our hands were peppered
With thorn pricks, our palms sticky as Bluebeard's.

We hoarded the fresh berries in the byre.
But when the bath was filled we found a fur,
A rat-grey fungus, glutting on our cache.
The juice was stinking too. Once off the bush
The fruit fermented, the sweet flesh would turn sour.
I always felt like crying. It wasn't fair
That all the lovely canfuls smelt of rot.
Each year I hoped they'd keep, knew they would not.

THE WIFE'S TALE

When I had spread it all on linen cloth
Under the hedge, I called them over.
The hum and gulp of the thresher ran down
And the big belt slewed to a standstill, straw
Hanging undelivered in the jaws.
There was such quiet that I heard their boots
Crunching the stubble twenty yards away.

He lay down and said 'Give these fellows theirs.
I'm in no hurry,' plucking grass in handfuls
And tossing it in the air. 'That looks well.'
(He nodded at my white cloth on the grass.)
'I declare a woman could lay out a field
Though boys like us have little call for cloths.'
He winked, then watched me as I poured a cup
And buttered the thick slices that he likes.
'It's threshing better than I thought, and mind
It's good clean seed. Away over there and look.'
Always this inspection has to be made
Even when I don't know what to look for.

But I ran my hand in the half-filled bags
Hooked to the slots. It was hard as shot,
Innumerable and cool. The bags gaped
Where the chutes ran back to the stilled drum
And forks were stuck at angles in the ground
As javelins might mark lost battlefields.
I moved between them back across the stubble.

They lay in the ring of their own crusts and dregs
Smoking and saying nothing. 'There's good yield,
Isn't there?' – as proud as if he were the land itself –
'Enough for crushing and for sowing both.'
And that was it. I'd come and he had shown me
So I belonged no further to the work.
I gathered cups and folded up the cloth
And went. But they still kept their ease
Spread out, unbuttoned, grateful, under the trees.

CHURNING DAY

A thick crust, coarse-grained as limestone rough-cast,
hardened gradually on top of the four crocks
that stood, large pottery bombs, in the small pantry.
After the hot brewery of gland, cud and udder
cool porous earthenware fermented the buttermilk
for churning day, when the hooped churn was scoured
with plumping kettles and the busy scrubber
echoed daintily on the seasoned wood.
It stood then, purified, on the flagged kitchen floor.

Out came the four crocks, spilled their heavy lip
of cream, their white insides, into the sterile churn.
The staff, like a great whisky muddler fashioned
in deal wood, was plunged in, the lid fitted.
My mother took first turn, set up rhythms
that slugged and thumped for hours. Arms ached.
Hands blistered. Cheeks and clothes were spattered
with flabby milk.

Where finally gold flecks
began to dance. They poured hot water then,
sterilized a birchwood-bowl
and little corrugated butter-spades.
Their short stroke quickened, suddenly
a yellow curd was weighting the churned up white,
heavy and rich, coagulated sunlight
that they fished, dripping, in a wide tin strainer,
heaped up like gilded gravel in the bowl.

The house would stink long after churning day,
acrid as a sulphur mine. The empty crocks
were ranged along the wall again, the butter
in soft printed slabs was piled on pantry shelves.
And in the house we moved with gravid ease,
our brains turned crystals full of clean deal churns,
the plash and gurgle of the sour-breathed milk,
the pat and slap of small spades on wet lumps.

DOCKER

There, in the corner, staring at his drink.
The cap juts like a gantry's crossbeam,
Cowling plated forehead and sledgehead jaw.
Speech is clamped in the lips' vice.

That fist would drop a hammer on a Catholic –
Oh yes, that kind of thing could start again;
The only Roman collar he tolerates
Smiles all round his sleek pint of porter.

Mosaic imperatives bang home like rivets;
God is a foreman with certain definite views
Who orders life in shifts of work and leisure.
A factory horn will blare the Resurrection.

He sits, strong and blunt as a Celtic cross,
Clearly used to silence and an armchair:
Tonight the wife and children will be quiet
At slammed door and smoker's cough in the hall.

THATCHER

Bespoke for weeks, he turned up some morning
Unexpectedly, his bicycle slung
With a light ladder and a bag of knives.
He eyed the old rigging, poked at the eaves,

Opened and handled sheaves of lashed wheat-straw.
Next, the bundled rods: hazel and willow
Were flicked for weight, twisted in case they'd snap.
It seemed he spent the morning warming up:

Then fixed the ladder, laid out well honed blades
And snipped at straw and sharpened ends of rods
That, bent in two, made a white-pronged staple
For pinning down his world, handful by handful.

Couchant for days on sods above the rafters
He shaved and flushed the butts, stitched all together
Into a sloped honeycomb, a stubble patch,
And left them gaping at his Midas touch.

THE DIVINER

Cut from the green hedge a forked hazel stick
That he held tight by the arms of the V:
Circling the terrain, hunting the pluck
Of water, nervous, but professionally

Unfussed. The pluck came sharp as a sting.
The rod jerked down with precise convulsions,
Spring water suddenly broadcasting
Through a green aerial its secret stations.

The bystanders would ask to have a try.
He handed them the rod without a word.
It lay dead in their grasp till nonchalantly
He gripped expectant wrists. The hazel stirred.

FOLLOWER

My father worked with a horse-plough,
His shoulders globed like a full sail strung
Between the shafts and the furrow.
The horses strained at his clicking tongue.

An expert. He would set the wing
And fit the bright steel-pointed sock.
The sod rolled over without breaking.
At the headrig, with a single pluck

Of reins, the sweating team turned round
And back into the land. His eye
Narrowed and angled at the ground,
Mapping the furrow exactly.

I stumbled in his hob-nailed wake,
Fell sometimes on the polished sod;
Sometimes he rode me on his back
Dipping and rising to his plod.

I wanted to grow up and plough,
To close one eye, stiffen my arm.
All I ever did was follow
In his broad shadow round the farm.

I was a nuisance, tripping, falling,
Yapping always. But today
It is my father who keeps stumbling
Behind me, and will not go away.

THE BARN

Threshed corn lay piled like grit of ivory
Or solid as cement in two-lugged sacks.
The musty dark hoarded an armoury
Of farmyard implements, harness, plough-socks.

The floor was mouse-grey, smooth, chilly concrete.
There were no windows, just two narrow shafts
Of gilded motes, crossing, from air-holes slit
High in each gable. The one door meant no draughts

All summer when the zinc burned like an oven.
A scythe's edge, a clean spade, a pitch-fork's prongs:
Slowly bright objects formed when you went in.
Then you felt cobwebs clogging up your lungs

And scuttled fast into the sunlit yard.
And into nights when bats were on the wing
Over the rafters of sleep, where bright eyes stared
From piles of grain in corners, fierce, unblinking.

The dark gulfed like a roof-space. I was chaff
To be pecked up when birds shot through the air-slits.
I lay face-down to shun the fear above.
The two-lugged sacks moved in like great blind rats.

PERSONAL HELICON

As a child, they could not keep me from wells
And old pumps with buckets and windlasses.
I loved the dark drop, the trapped sky, the smells
Of waterweed, fungus and dank moss.

One, in a brickyard, with a rotted board top.
I savoured the rich crash when a bucket
Plummeted down at the end of a rope.
So deep you saw no reflection in it.

A shallow one under a dry stone ditch
Fructified like any aquarium.
When you dragged out long roots from the soft mulch
A white face hovered over the bottom.

Others had echoes, gave back your own call
With a clean new music in it. And one
Was scaresome for there, out of ferns and tall
Foxgloves, a rat slapped across my reflection.

Now, to pry into roots, to finger slime,
To stare big-eyed Narcissus, into some spring
Is beneath all adult dignity. I rhyme
To see myself, to set the darkness echoing.

SERENADES

The Irish nightingale
Is a sedge-warbler,
A little bird with a big voice
Kicking up a racket all night.

Not what you'd expect
From the musical nation.
I haven't even heard one –
Nor an owl, for that matter.

My serenades have been
The broken voice of a crow
In a draught or a dream,
The wheeze of bats

Or the ack-ack
Of the tramp corncrake
Lost in a no man's land
Between combines and chemicals.

So fill the bottles, love,
Leave them inside their cots.
And if they do wake us, well,
So would the sedge-warbler.

LIMBO

Fishermen at Ballyshannon
Netted an infant last night
Along with the salmon.
An illegitimate spawning,

A small one thrown back
To the waters. But I'm sure
As she stood in the shallows
Ducking him tenderly

Till the frozen knobs of her wrists
Were dead as the gravel,
He was a minnow with hooks
Tearing her open.

She waded in under
The sign of her cross.
He was hauled in with the fish.
Now limbo will be

A cold glitter of souls
Through some far briny zone.
Even Christ's palms, unhealed,
Smart and cannot fish there.

SHORELINE

Turning a corner, taking a hill
In County Down, there's the sea
Sidling and settling to
The back of a hedge. Or else

A grey bottom with puddles
Dead-eyed as fish.
Haphazard tidal craters march
The corn and the grazing.

All round Antrim and westward
Two hundred miles at Moher
Basalt stands to.
Both ocean and channel

Froth at the black locks
On Ireland. And strands
Take hissing submissions
Off Wicklow and Mayo.

Take any minute. A tide
Is rummaging in
At the foot of all fields,
All cliffs and shingles.

Listen. Is it the Danes,
A black hawk bent on the sail?
Or the chinking Normans?
Or currachs hopping high

On to the sand?
Strangford, Arklow, Carrickfergus,
Belmullet and Ventry
Stay, forgotten like sentries.

BOGLAND

We have no prairies
To slice a big sun at evening –
Everywhere the eye concedes to
Encroaching horizon,

Is wooed into the cyclops' eye
Of a tarn. Our unfenced country
Is bog that keeps crusting
Between the sights of the sun.

They've taken the skeleton
Of the Great Irish Elk
Out of the peat, set it up
An astounding crate full of air.

Butter sunk under
More than a hundred years
Was recovered salty and white.
The ground itself is kind, black butter

Melting and opening underfoot,
Missing its last definition
By millions of years.
They'll never dig coal here,

Only the waterlogged trunks
Of great firs, soft as pulp.
Our pioneers keep striking
Inwards and downwards,

Every layer they strip
Seems camped on before.
The bogholes might be Atlantic seepage.
The wet centre is bottomless.

THE TOLLUND MAN

I

Some day I will go to Aarhus
To see his peat-brown head,
The mild pods of his eye-lids,
His pointed skin cap.

In the flat country nearby
Where they dug him out,
His last gruel of winter seeds
Caked in his stomach,

Naked except for
The cap, noose and girdle,
I will stand a long time.
Bridegroom to the goddess,

She tightened her torc on him
And opened her fen,
Those dark juices working
Him to a saint's kept body,

Trove of the turfcutters'
Honeycombed workings.
Now his stained face
Reposes at Aarhus.

II

I could risk blasphemy,
Consecrate the cauldron bog
Our holy ground and pray
Him to make germinate

The scattered, ambushed
Flesh of labourers,
Stockinged corpses
Laid out in the farmyards,

Tell-tale skin and teeth
Flecking the sleepers
Of four young brothers, trailed
For miles along the lines.

III

Something of his sad freedom
As he rode the tumbril
Should come to me, driving,
Saying the names

Tollund, Grabaulle, Nebelgard,
Watching the pointing hands
Of country people,
Not knowing their tongue.

Out there in Jutland
In the old man-killing parishes
I will feel lost,
Unhappy and at home.

BOG QUEEN

I lay waiting
between turf-face and demesne wall,
between heathery levels
and glass-toothed stone.

My body was braille
for the creeping influences:
dawn suns groped over my head
and cooled at my feet,

through my fabrics and skins
the seeps of winter
digested me,
the illiterate roots

pondered and died
in the cavings
of stomach and sockets.
I lay waiting

on the gravel bottom,
my brain darkening,
a jar of bog-spawn
fermenting underground

dreams of Baltic amber.
Bruised berries under my nails,
the vital hoard reducing
in the crock of the pelvis.

My diadem grew carious,
gemstones dropped
in the peat floe
like bearings of history.

My sash was a black glacier
wrinkling, dyed weaves
and phoenician stitchwork
retted on my breasts'

soft moraines.
I knew winter cold
like the nuzzle of fjords
at my thighs –

the soaked fledge,
the swaddle of hides.
My skull hibernated
in the wet nest of my hair.

Which they robbed.
I was barbered
and stripped
by a turfcutter's spade

who veiled me again
and packed coomb
softly between stone jambs
at my head and my feet.

Till a peer's wife bribed him.
The plait of my hair,
a slimy birth-cord
of bog, had been cut

and I rose from the dark,
hacked bone, skull-ware,
frayed stitches, tufts,
small gleams on the bank.

Robert Morgan

Author's Introduction

I was born in the Cynon Valley, South Wales, a deep, narrow valley with a poisoned river, railway sidings with coal trucks, and terraced cottages perched on the mountain side. There were seven coal mines within sight from the cottage where I lived.

My father worked as a coal miner for fifty years. His father and grandfather had also been coal miners, so it seemed natural that I should become a miner. To me, at fourteen, the mine was an Aladdin's cave with fairy lights. I began work in the mine two days after I left school, and I stayed a miner until the ripe age of twenty-six.

Those twelve years in the earth's hive, working like a mole in the dark in a seam two feet thick, left their marks upon me, some of which can never be erased. There are memories of pit life I cherish, and some I try to forget.

I wrote when I was a miner, not poems, but short stories, some of which were published when I was still a miner. I began writing poems years after I left the mine. I must have written over a hundred and fifty poems connected with mines and miners. In such poems I recalled the experiences of the lamplit mine where I worked. I wrote of the dangers, the comradeship, the tragedy of accidents, the terraced cottages and derelict mines. I wrote of the landscape decorated with slag heaps and pit-gears.

Over the last decade I have been involved in the teaching of mentally handicapped children, and I have dipped into this experience for poems. I now live in an English village where I am absorbing the countryside's landscape of trees, wild flowers, animals and bird life, and these things are also influencing my work. 'Nightwatchman' is a poem connected with a new kind of experience, far removed from that of mining.

I suppose I could be labelled an autobiographical poet, as I write directly from my personal experiences, and as I am not able to shed completely my early experiences as a miner I still write the occasional mining poem.

I have been asked on many occasions why do I write poetry, and

I give a different answer each time, depending on the particular mood I'm in. This question is immensely difficult to answer, for I'm not really sure myself why I write poetry. I know for certain it is a very difficult art to practise, for each poem I write is a hard slog to put 'the right words in the right order'. And it doesn't get any easier. I must have written altogether about three hundred poems, and I cannot remember one that's been easy to write. So why do I write poetry you may ask? Perhaps the answer lies in the poems I write. I hope so; for the risk of giving the wrong impression, through a prose definition, is too great.

BIRTH OF A POET

He stood at the window
Staring at the metal-torn earth,
Free, at last, of the pit's toil.

What could he say
After fifty years a miner?
What could he take
From the mine's darkness?

His hand gripped the delicate pen.
He wrote the words slowly, remembering
All the images of sweat and blood.

BLACK RAILINGS

There were black railings.
Beyond the railings a river
And further still a mine,
Like shanties in a mist.

This was the scene that Tudor saw
Through the window above his desk.
He'd seen it many times before
But that morning his watching pose
Was like a sculpture stillness
As if his bitterness had grown cold.

We kept a nervous vigilance
With books until the crack of chalk
In Tudor's hand disturbed
Our self-imposed silence.

When the hour hooter blew
Across the valley nave
It signalled from the mine
Where Tudor's brother,
Days before, had perished
In the dark and savage earth.

BLOOD DONOR

The searching was easy and memory ripens
On the grey earth picture of Rees
In his grimy vest soaked in blood.
Forty-eight years under tense rock
Had stripped him like a tree with roots
In slag and marked him with texture of strain
And accident. But it was slow legs
And dust-worn eyes that were to blame.

The iron rock-bar was still in his hands
Held like a spear of a fallen warrior.
The rocks had dyed his silver hair red
And the heavy bar was warm and worn.
Blind flies swarmed in the blood-sweat
Air and the tough men with bruised
Senses were gentle, using distorted
Hands like women arranging flowers.

On the way out through roads of rocky
Silence you could sense images of confusion
In the slack chain of shadows. Muscles
Were nerve-tight and thoughts infested

With wrath and sharp edges of fear.
Towards the sun's lamp we moved, taking
Home the dark prisoner in his shroud of coats.

MEN IN BLACK

The men in black with pit faces
Of skin tight over tough bones
Stand under a grey loaded sky
In the shade of a black mountain.
Words of David fall on their ears
And bend them with fear and mystery.
The reader in white unmoved and neutral
Breaks the last link between them
And the young man in the earth of Wales.
When the black cars sneak away
The yard settles to its cold silence
With a new sleeper from Cynon Pit.

BOOK OF STONES

For ten decades this river has crawled
In black with pit-poison and blood
On a scarred landscape under a Welsh sky.
There are no sheep on the dead hills of
Sharp slag lifted by distorted hands
From dark places deep in broken earth.
Industrial Readymades darken the sky
And pit-ponds green and calm
Lap beaches of desolate ash.
Wry trees break with brittle cries
In the dust-wind over tombstones of men.
These men, buried with silica scars,
Lie hidden with the same cold rock
Marked long ago by their warm hands.
Their plain history in the Book of Stones,
Now eroded by the wind's work, is unknown
Or forgotten.
Where is their memorial?
They gathered the brute harvest deep
In the vaults of earth and made men rich.

FREE COAL

He was picking coal from a tip
When I passed his bent back.
His small daughter squatted
Beside a half filled sack,
Holding it against the slope
Of the dribbling slag.
The sky was younger then
And life was a bowl of shadows
In a valley of faded days,
And I was too young for the mask
Of depression which that man carried
On his thin, unemployed face.

DERELICT VALLEY

Come this way through Autumn streets
And see the black river gurgling
Around hill skirts embroidered with tombs
Of disused poetry and music. See that man
Feeding pigeons in a garden of frozen
Footprints and a woman searching a chapel
In a hymn silence under broken windows.
Remember the miners coughing in a morning
Mist and remember the pit-widows waiting
With knitting and photographs and a silver
Piece for luck. See the empty front-room shops
Where mints, homemade toffee and cakes
Decorated the sun's light in days dressed
For memory. See the hushed cottages
Stiff with dreams and cold grates black
With birds. There are no coal-trucks
Under schoolboy bridges but cones of slag
Still pierce the memorial sky. In a mean room
In the Workmen's Hall twilight miners
Play dominoes on the edge of Heaven,
Their hands and faces wrought with tapestry
Of rock and toil. The pits are closed
And deep down in the squeezed hives
Men's history of spilled blood
Is chronicled in silent darkness.

The tea is cold and the young
Have gone over the hills. But listen . . .
The history of this place is not silent.
You can hear music from the lips of the night
As the wheel of memory turns back
To harmonies of political streets
And rolling words rich with a pride
Of psalms. Listen . . . children's voices
Are calling and Cynon men are singing
And lovers plan in bluebell woods.
But let us go now. It is all fading
And night is shading forever moments
Etching invisible patterns on this
Landscape that was once a symphony of men
Set in a tone of dark plunder in a valley
Pledged to work. Webs of pit-gear
Freeze against the stars and the withered
Slopes are branded with danger.
A dog barks against the silence
And the tinsel moon shivers on the river.
But let us go now,
This way, to the road over the hills.

VALLEY

Packed streets, humbled by the
Mercy of music, sprawl
On windribbed slopes.
A pit-infested river snakewalks
Between hills fouled by slag
And the piece of eternal sky
Is written with a century of dreams
In language of invaded earth.

In this roofless nave endemic
Dust sparkles on the sun's
Apron, intrepid men return
From mines, quiescent men,
Eloquent with time and toil,
Sit badgered by dreams in sanctuary
Of silence. In patches of woods
Warriors have cursed Roman

Wounds and tree packed quarries have
Echoed the monk's chisel.

Memories grow here, miraged
In timeless air vibrant
With the sun's magic . . . and I have
Returned like an intruder ambushed
By the shadows of the past.

THE CWM ABOVE PENRHIWCEIBER

There was sparkling water, too small
For a river, too big for a stream.
As boys we sampled it as early
As April when the weather changed.
We dammed it and dived off a tree
And gasped in the trout-cold water.
We crept through dark growth
Of young and old trees, tall
Fern and tangled bramble where the sun
Could only get fingers through.
The ground sagged under foot
And bird and insect silence
Was rich with arrows of history.
Ghosts sighed in a trapped
Breeze and every indigo shadow
Hid a skeleton and a sword.
Out in the sunlight we shouted
Our fears away and romped home,
Glancing back at our Cwm
Now buried under rubbish from pits.

HUW'S FARM

Up at Huw's farm nature
Is invading gently, fingering
Its way over a wilderness of deserted
Relics. Here, Huw, Rachel
And two sons once toiled
On a bare hill blotted
With cones of slag and memories.
Now shattered windows grin

Under creeping green locks
And the rude wind mocks
The empty rooms inhabited
By the curious sad silence of
Vanished people and homely residue.
Out in the brambled yard a rust
Crippled plough is sinking into
Forgotten soil and a toppled
Dry wall lets in the tide of
Couch grass from the hill breast.
Down in the valley, pits,
Vague through dust and smoke,
Whisper the dark fugue of
Industry and stubborn faith
Under a chapel eye of God.

THE STRANGERS

The strangers have vanished –
Two, aged, inseparable Edwardians,
A lady and a gentleman,
Dated by their wardrobe.
They had lived behind hedges
And trees in a flint cottage
Untouched by t.v. and car.

They were seen occasionally
Walking slowly and elegantly
In the sun, a curious pair
In black from an album world
Of bible, lace and gramophone.
They retreated from our tinsel
World of prosperity, and we,
Their strangers, came in from
The city with children and car
To live in the country and disturb
A century of tranquillity.

I passed the flint cottage many times,
And passing glanced between two bars
Of a locked gate, the only space
In a massive hedge spilling over
A flint wall bent by hungry roots.
A weed path led to the cottage
Wreathed in ivy, lichen and dust.

One summer day I climbed into the garden
Where a lawn, deep in seeding grass,
Was spreading four ways under the boughs
Of a great oak and beyond under sycamores
And sumacs statuelike and geometric
Against the sky. I felt the uninhabited
Stillness and the strange air of time past
Stirring in the quiet friction of foliage . . .
And I heard, from gaping windows, the cry
Of hollow rooms . . . The residue of human
Habitation lay scattered like leaves
Of a dozen Autumns, and an arch of roses
Hung like spirals of barbed wire.

Beyond this barrier I stood
In a darker region where the sun
Simmered behind a green canopy
With shafts of silver light.
A summer-house of shadows
And fungus lay trapped
In an arena of green time.
A tree, cut close to earth,
And a fallen, rustic table,
Were sinking into waves of grass.
They were requisites for tea
On the lawn – broken mirrors
For a glance at silhouettes.

I listened to the little sounds –
The interpreters of a derelict place
And over my shoulder four shattered
Rectangles, with ivy teeth, seemed like
A monster guarding a sanctuary
Of frozen reality . . . I retreated
And emerged at the road, drenched
By dark references of a lost age.

ASYLUM FOR WAR VICTIMS

Inside these walls
Men are strange and detached.
Only the mind's
Occasional earthquake
Of guns, and the scream
Of a scuttled body,
Make them pause
Like a flicker of sanity.

On wet days they play
With psychological toys,
Fumble with absent-minded fingers
And grin like clowns.

Some do not play but linger
Among the shavings of reality.
They are led from chair to chair,
From table to bed.

They are war's most strange
Somnambulists, like statues
Adrift from pedestals.

They have the privacy
Of a country mansion
And there are beautiful gardens
Where they take supervised exercise
Among the meaningless flowers.

CHAMPION

Billy was a marble champion
With cord for a belt
And elbow holes in his jersey.

We played an hour before school
On the concrete playground.
But he dashed all our glassies

Out of the chalk ring,
Then he'd sell his winnings
And buy breakfast at lunchtime.

THE ART LESSON

They do not paint a still-life
Or a country scene but a skull,
A side view of a long haired
Youth in a long jacket
And a thin knife tipped with red.
These are class symbols, the clandestine
Snaps from subnormal minds groping.
Their strong, grimed, manlike hands
Trace the disturbances, releasing signs
Of a potential and setting light to areas
Unmapped by doctors and schoolmasters.
They are proud of their symbols.
Van Gogh's slashed ear in brown paper
Sets a thrill vibrating in the prison
Of their dangers.

But they paint the
Truth for me; their colours and lines
Are sincere, for their works have no
Formulas to make them pretty; they
Are intuitive and absolutely creative.

DICKENS CHARACTERS

They are restless. Their blood flows with anger
And compulsions. Their stern eyes are dark
With confusion. Their growing bones cry out
Against the boundaries of desks and walls.
They tolerate my voice vibrating with education,
But they find no fault with me,
Only what I do for a living.
And what I do must be done according to the law.
They want to join me on the old road
Of knowledge, but they will only stare at shadows,
Lose themselves among the strange turnings,
And hesitate too long at bare places
Trodden by toughs and killers.
Their imaginations are distorted by violence,
Pre-natal interference, cold homes, and by failure
Created by our system which pigeonholes brains
Into grades A, B, and C. I squeeze words hard.
But they lean against them. I squeeze harder,
Trying to reach their personalities and beyond
To the corners of imaginations still bright
With silver thoughts and joys of discovery.
I pause. The silences are places where we can meet,
Or retreat, or hear an inner voice,
Or pray for a second chance with success . . .
'Listen boys . . . the workhouse was a place
Where Oliver was born . . . there were such places
All over England not so long ago . . .
It was a place to go when you were destitute.'
Jackson in the front desk leans forward.
He has free dinners, a prostitute sister,
A neurotic mother and his father is a stranger.
I read a passage on the workhouse boys
And show pictures from my old copy.
They leave their desks and examine the pictures.
Questions are asked and answered and we linger

Over the pictures and wonder. The playtime bells
Ring in the corridors and they leave slowly,
Taking with them vague thoughts of England's
Workhouses and a boy without parents.
Jackson stays behind with the book.
He knows Oliver Twist far better than I.

NIGHTWATCHMAN

He scans a nocturnal acre for prey.

When he calls his hoot-voice
Charges through night's dark
And night's silence.

It is like an ambush.
I hear it when sleep
Does not come easily.

Out there his eyes filter darkness
And a ripple in the grass
Moves the angle of his beak.

When he moves there is no sound
And his stone-drop is timed
To a grass-blade's shudder.

In the wood's dark stillness
He rips and tears
For his lonely meal.

After the kill he rises
As lightly as gossamer
To his watching post.

Then he calls when I am most vulnerable.

THE CHOICE

They were landing and the great thrust
Pressed like magnetism on their bodies.
The silver ship hovered then slowly
Dropped on meadow grass.

Starglyn, the captain, stared
At the green landscape.
Between two hills a deserted city,
Crumbling and overgrown, patterned
The Scanning Screen. The dials
On the Blue Screen indicated
No human life present.

Suncon, the Celestial Geologist,
Smiled over his captain's shoulder.

'You were right,' said Starglyn.
'They must have been a very aggressive people.
What was your main source of information?'

'The great meteorite which broke
From Earth in 2048 A.D.
We took it to Station Z
And examined it.
It told us everything.'

'What?' asked Starglyn.

'They were allowed to choose
Between good and evil
And they chose evil . . .'

'Bloody fools,' muttered Starglyn.

Leslie Norris

Author's Introduction

The Scots have a word for the poet; they call him a 'makar', or maker. I think this a much more meaningful term than the word we use, since it places the poet firmly beside all the other makers, all the other craftsmen. It was the great Irish poet, W. B. Yeats, who gave this advice to the young poets of his country – 'Sing whatever is well made' – and it is the best advice I know. After the first exhilarating moments of inspiration, then the writing of poetry is laborious, intricate, eminently satisfying when you get it right.

But 'makar' implies more than a mere skill at the craft of words, important as this is. It means that the words themselves must actually *make* whatever it is you are writing about. By their sounds, by the differing emphasis each word takes in the line, by the spaces at the ends of lines and between the stanzas, the words and shapes that make the poem must *make*, whole and complete, that bit of the world you are celebrating. In the early poem, 'The Ballad of Billy Rose', I have tried to make the whole fight visible and audible again; in the recent poem 'Barn Owl' I have tried to make the bird complete from his skeleton outward, so that he can fly again among us. What the poet does, it seems to me, is to make an alternative world, both for himself and for those who will listen to him.

Everybody who uses language is a poet at some time or another. It is the thing that we use language for most completely. All we have to do is look so carefully at the world we experience, to know its sounds and its textures as well as its appearances so well, that we have to find the words to recreate the intensity of what we know.

A GIRL'S SONG

Early one morning
As I went out walking
I saw the young sailor
Go fresh through the fields.
His eye was as blue as
The sky up above us
And clean was his skin
As the colour of shells.

O where are you going,
Young sailor, so early?
And may I come with you
A step as you go?
He looked with his eye
And I saw the deep sea-tombs,
He opened his mouth
And I heard the sea roar.

And limp on his head
Lay his hair green as sea-grass
And scrubbed were his bones
By the inching of sand.
The long tides enfolded
The lines of his body
And slow corals grow
At the stretch of his hand.

I look from my window
In the first light of morning
And I look from my door
At the dark of the day,
But all that I see are
The fields flat and empty
And the black road run down
To Cardigan town.

A SMALL WAR

Climbing from Merthyr through the dew of August mornings
When I was a centaur-cyclist, on the skills of wheels
I'd loop past the Storey Arms, past streaming lorries
Stopped for flasks of early tea, and fall into Breconshire.
A thin road under black Fan Frynych – which keeps its winter
Shillings long through Spring – took me to the Senni valley.

That was my plenty, to rest on the narrow saddle
Looking down on the farms, letting the simple noises
Come singly up. It was there I saw a ring-ousel
Wearing the white gash of his mountains; but every
Sparrow's feather in that valley was rare, golden,
Perfect. It was an Eden fourteen miles from home.

Evan Drew, my second cousin, lived there, a long, slow man
With a brown gaze I remember him. From a hill farm
Somewhere on the slopes above Heol Senni he sent his sons,
Boys a little older than I, to the second World War.
They rode their ponies to the station, they waved
Goodbye, they circled the spitting sky above Europe.

I would not fight for Wales, the great battle-cries
Do not arouse me. I keep short boundaries holy,
Those my eyes have recognized and my heart has known
As welcome. Nor would I fight for her language. I spend
My few pence of Welsh to amuse my friends, to comment
On the weather. They carry no thought that could be mine.

It's the small wars I understand. So now that forty
People lock their gates in Senni, keeping the water out
With frailest barriers of love and anger, I'd fight for them.
Five miles of land, enough small farms to make a heaven,
Are easily trapped on the drawing-board, a decision
Of the pen drowns all. Yes, the great towns need

The humming water, yes, I have taken my rods to other
Swimming valleys and happily fished above the vanished
Fields. I know the arguments. It is a handful of earth
I will not argue with, and the slow cattle swinging weightily
Home. When I open the taps in my English bathroom
I am surprised they do not run with Breconshire blood.

JULY THE SEVENTH

Drugged all day, the summer
Flagged in its heat, brutal
Weather sullen as brass.
There was no comfort in darkness.
Hotter than breath we lay

On beds too warm for moving,
Near open windows. Full of
Spaces the house was, walls
Fretting for a brisk air.
A door slammed flat in its

Loud frame, banging us awake.
Wind was bringing in the storm.
Quick switches of whipped light
Flicked the rooftops, made shadowless
The ends of rooms. The stopped clock

Marked the lightning. I got up
Heavily, shut the house against
Thunder. Rain was a long time
Coming, then sparse drops, stinging
Like metal, hit the bricks, the hot

Pavements. When it sweetened
To plenty, the streets tamed it,
Flowed it in pipes and conduits,
Channelled it underground through
Stony runnels. The rain brought

So faint a smell of hay I searched
My mind for it, thinking it memory.
I lay freshly awake on the cool sheets,
Hearing the storm. Somewhere, far off,
Cut grass lay in files, the hay spoiling.

THE BALLAD OF BILLY ROSE

Outside Bristol Rovers' Football Ground –
The date has gone from me, but not the day,
Nor how the dissenting flags in stiff array
Struck bravely out against the sky's grey round –

Near the Car Park then, past Austin and Ford,
Lagonda, Bentley, and a colourful patch
Of country coaches come in for the match,
Was where I walked, having travelled the road

From Fishponds to watch Portsmouth in the Cup,
The Third Round, I believe. And I was filled
With the old excitement which had thrilled
Me so completely when, while growing up,

I went on Saturdays to match or fight.
Not only me; for thousands of us there
Strode forward eagerly, each man aware
Of tingling memory, anticipating delight.

We all marched forward, all, except one man.
I saw him because he was paradoxically still,
A stone against the flood, face upright against us all,
Head bare, hoarse voice aloft, blind as a stone.

I knew him at once, despite his pathetic clothes;
Something in his stance, or his sturdy frame
Perhaps. I could even remember his name
Before I saw it on his blind-man's tray. Billy Rose.

And twenty forgetful years fell away at the sight.
Bare-kneed, dismayed, memory fled to the hub
Of Saturday violence, with friends to the Labour Club,
Watching the boxing on a sawdust summer night.

The boys' enclosure close to the shabby ring
Was where we stood, clenched in a resin world,
Spoke in cool voices, lounged, were artificially bored
During minor bouts. We paid threepence to go in.

Billy Rose fought there. He was top of the bill.
So brisk a fighter, so gallant, so precise!
Trim as a tree he stood for the ceremonies,
Then turned to meet George Morgan of Tirphil.

He had no chance. Courage was not enough,
Nor tight defence. Donald Davies was sick
And we threatened his cowardice with an embarrassed kick.
Ripped across both his eyes was Rose, but we were tough

And clapped him as they wrapped his blindness up
In busy towels, applauded the wave
He gave his executioners, cheered the brave
Blind man as he cleared with a jaunty hop

The top rope. I had forgotten that day
As if it were dead for ever, yet now I saw
The flowers of punched blood on the ring floor,
As bright as his name. I do not know

How long I stood with ghosts of the wild fists
And the cries of shaken boys long dead around me,
For struck to act at last, in terror and pity
I threw some frantic money, three treacherous pence –

And I cry at the memory – into his tray, and ran,
Entering the waves of the stadium like a drowning man.
Poor Billy Rose. God, he could fight,
Before my three sharp coins knocked out his sight.

WATER

On hot summer mornings my aunt set glasses
On a low wall outside the farmhouse,
With some jugs of cold water.
I would sit in the dark hall, or
        Behind the dairy window,
Waiting for children to come from the town.

They came in small groups, serious, steady,
And I could see them, black in the heat,
Long before they turned in at our gate
To march up the soft, dirt road.
        They would stand by the wall,
Drinking water with an engrossed thirst. The dog

Did not bother them, knowing them responsible
Travellers. They held in quiet hands their bags
Of jam sandwiches, and bottles of yellow fizz.
Sometimes they waved a gratitude to the house,
        But they never looked at us.
Their eyes were full of the mountain, lifting

Their measuring faces above our long hedge.
When they had gone I would climb the wall,
Looking for them among the thin sheep runs.
Their heads were a resolute darkness among ferns,
        They climbed with unsteady certainty.
I wondered what it was they knew the mountain had.

They would pass the last house, Lambert's, where
A violent gander, too old by many a Christmas,
Blared evil warning from his bitten moor,
Then it was open world, too high and clear
        For clouds even, where over heather
The free hare cleanly ran, and the summer sheep.

I knew this; and I knew all summer long
Those visionary gangs passed through our lanes,
Coming down at evening, their arms full
Of cowslips, moon daisies, whinberries, nuts,
        All fruits of the sliding seasons,
And the enormous experience of the mountain

That I who loved it did not understand.
In the summer, dust filled our winter ruts
With a level softness, and children walked
At evening through golden curtains scuffed
        From the road by their trailing feet.
They would drink tiredly at our wall, talking

Softly, leaning, their sleepy faces warm for home.
We would see them murmur slowly through our stiff
Gate, their shy heads gilded by the last sun.
One by one we would gather up the used jugs,
        The glasses. We would pour away
A little water. It would lie on the thick dust, gleaming.

BARN OWL

Ernie Morgan found him, a small
Fur mitten inexplicably upright,
And hissing like a treble kettle
Beneath the tree he'd fallen from.
His bright eye frightened Ernie,
Who popped a rusty bucket over him

And ran for us. We kept him
In a backyard shed, perched
On the rung of a broken deck-chair,
Its canvas faded to his down's biscuit.
Men from the pits, their own childhood
Spent waste in the crippling earth,
Held him gently, brought him mice
From the wealth of our riddled tenements,
Saw that we understood his tenderness,
His tiny body under its puffed quilt,
Then left us alone. We called him Snowy.

He was never clumsy. He flew
From the first like a skilled moth,
Sifting the air with feathers,
Floating it softly to the place he wanted.
At dusk he'd stir, preen, stand
At the window-ledge, fly. It was
A catching of the heart to see him go.
Six months we kept him, saw him
Grow beautiful in a way each thought
His own knowledge. One afternoon, home
With pretended illness, I watched him
Leave. It was daylight. He lifted slowly
Over the Hughes's roof, his cream face calm,
And never came back. I saw this;
And tell it for the first time,
Having wanted to keep his mystery.

And would not say it now, but that
This morning, walking in Slindon woods
Before the sun, I found a barn owl
Dead in the rusty bracken.
He was not clumsy in his death,
His wings folded decently to him,
His plumes, unruffled orange,
Bore flawlessly their delicate patterning.
With a stick I turned him, not
Wishing to touch his feathery stiffness.
There was neither blood nor wound on him,
But for the savaged foot a scavenger
Had ripped. I saw the sinews.
I could have skewered them out
Like a common fowl's. Moving away

I was oppressed by him, thinking
Confusedly that down the generations
Of air this death was Snowy's
Emblematic messenger, that I should know
The meaning of it, the dead barn owl.

OWLS

The owls are flying. From hedge to hedge
Their deep-mouthed voices call the fields
Of England, stretching north and north,
To a sibilant hunt above ditches;
And small crawlers, bent in crevices, yield
Juice of their threaded veins, with

A small kernel of bones. It was earlier
I walked the lace of the sea at this south
Edge, walked froths of the fallen moon
Bare-legged in the autumn water
So cold it set my feet like stones
In its inches, and I feel on breath

And ankles the touch of the charged sea
Since. I saw in my lifting eyes the flat
Of this one country, north stretching,
And north. I saw its hills, the public light
Of its cities, and every blatant tree
Burning, with assembled autumn burning.

I know the same sun, in a turn
Of earth, will bring morning, grey
As gulls or mice to us. And I know
In my troubled night the owls fly
Over us, wings wide as England,
And their voices will never go away.

BUZZARD

With infinitely confident little variations of his finger-ends
He soothes the erratic winds.
He hangs on air's gap, then turns
On royal wing into his untouchable circle.

All, all, lie under his sifting eye,
The squat man, the sheep, the mouse in the slate cleft.

He is not without pity for he does not know pity.
He is a machine for killing; searchlight eye,
Immaculate wing, then talon and hook.
He kills without cruelty for he does not know cruelty.

If he fails in a small death he is awkward. And angry,
Loosing upon the hills his terrible, petulant cry.
To fail often is to die.
His livelihood is such single-minded and obsessional artistry.

He is not seduced by emotion
Or impeccable clear thought even
Into considerations other than his pure life.

We observe our prey doubtfully,
Behind many hedges and in tufted country.
Even when we see it clear
Have too many words to kill it.

NIGHTINGALES

I

My namesake, old Bill Norris, standing beneath a tree
So bitterly gnarled he might have grown from it, stopped
Talking to listen, lifted eyes dayblue and delighted,
And laughed a silent pleasure. 'There's a good many,'
He said, 'Walks past as close as you and never hears her,
Though she sings as bright in the hot noon as any night.'
Two feet above his head the dun bird pulsed and lilted.
It was in this village and perhaps for this same bird
I lay awake the whole of one miraculous darkness.
She sang so close to my house I could have touched
Her singing; I could not breathe through the aching silences.
And for nights after, hunched among pillows, I grabbed
At any sleep at all, hearing the nightingale
Hammer my plaintive rest with remorseless melody.
Full of resented ecstasy, I groaned nightlong in my bed.

II

Or driving one Sunday morning in Maytime Hampshire
On our way to a christening in one of the villages,
We stopped on Steep Hill, the road climbing headily upwards.
In the first warm air of the year we looked down on the
Trees, unmoving and full in the freshness of their leaves.
There were eight nightingales, eight, they filled the valley
With sobbing, the cataracts of their voices fell
Erratically among the splendid beeches. Open-eyed
We stood on the lip of the hill, while near and far
The water-notes of their singing grew faint, were lost almost,
Answered and redoubled near at hand, trailed
Dropping sadly down the valley-sides, struck purely out
With sound round notes into the listening morning.
We were still with music, as the day was. That we were late
For the christening was to the credit of those nightingales.

III

When I was very young my father took me from bed,
Dressed me in haste, and we walked into the night.
Winter was so long gone I had forgotten darkness.
We went by paths which in daylight knew me well,
But now were strange with shadow. It was not long
Before we came to the wood where the nightingale sang,
The unbelievable bird who lived in the stories
Of almost my every book. Would it sing, would it sing?
I thought the wood was full of silent listeners.
I do not remember it singing. My father carried me home,
My head rolling back on its stalk at every measure
Of his deep stride, and all I have brought back
From that long night are the fixed stars reeling.
It is the poet's bird, they say. Perhaps I took it home,
For here I am, raising my voice, scraping my throat raw again.

CURLEW

Dropped from the air at evening, this desolate call
Mocks us, who listen to its delicate non-humanity.
Dogs smile, cats flatter, cows regard us all
With eyes like those of ladies in a city,

So that we transfer to them familiar human virtues
To comfort and keep us safe. But this adamant bird

With the plaintive throat and curved, uneasy jaws
Crying creates a desert with a word

More terrible than chaos, and we stand at the edge
Of nothing. How shall we know its purpose, this wild bird,
Whose world is not confined by the linnets' hedge,
Whose mouth lets fly the appalling cry we heard?

LAST LEAVES

Late last night, the moon in puddles, I walked the lane
North from my gate up to the small wood where,
Stirring and trembling from the sentient trees,
The last leaves fell. I heard them in the still air
Snap. And almost saw their sifting passage down
To join their squelching fellows on the ground,
All glory gone. I tread on the black wreck
Of the year. Well, it is over.
Here, in full arboreal summer, struck
By the squinting light, I took for a hawk
No more than a flapping pigeon. I'll not make
That mistake in valid winter. No. I'll see
Each full-eyed owl stir not a breath
Of frost among the visible twigs as he pads
On air; and remember the owl's truth
For the vole, the silver frog, and the
Soft-bellied mouse, her summer breeding done.

OCTOBER IN THE LANE

October in the lane, and the thin harebells,
Ghosts of their deep Augusts, pine in the hedges.
Puffed leaves thicken the crawling ditches
And tired wasps labour in the air,

Heavy with dying. Our trees prepare
The black calligraphies of winter, we strip
Our fields for the frost fire. Now roses drop
From the wall their falls of petals

And cheat my eyes with snowflakes. Smells
Of marauding weather come coldly in with the dark.

I remember a spring of snow that fell without mark
On my head and white hurry as I thudded for home

And we laughed to see how soon I became,
In a falling minute, a seven year old, white-haired man.
In the kitchen mirror I watched the quick years run
From the warm, and I wiped from my head

The unready white my April time pretended.
So many weathers have spread their tempers near me
That empty winters stretch behind my mirror
And the keenest razor will not shift their snowfalls.

EARLY FROST

We were warned about frost, yet all day the summer
Has wavered its heat above the empty stubble. Late
Bees hung their blunt weight,
Plump drops between those simplest wings, their leisure
An ignorance of frost.
My mind is full of the images of summer
And a liquid curlew calls from alps of air;

But the frost has come. Already under trees
Pockets of summer are dying, wide paths
Of the cold glow clean through the stricken thickets
And again I feel on my cheek the cut of winters
Dead. Once I awoke in a dark beyond moths
To a world still with freezing,
Hearing my father go to the yard for his ponies,

His hands full of frostnails to point their sliding
To a safe haul. I went to school,
Socks pulled over shoes for the streets' clear glass,
The early shops cautious, the tall
Classroom windows engraved by winter's chisel,
Fern, feather and flower that would not let the pale
Day through. We wrote in a cold fever for the morning

Play. Then boys in the exulting yard, ringing
Boots hard on winter, slapped with their polishing
Caps the arrows of their gliding, in steaming lines
Ran till they launched one by one

On the skills of ice their frail balance,
Sliding through life with not a fall in mind,
Their voices crying freely through such shouting

As the cold divided. I slid in the depth
Of the season till the swung bell sang us in.
Now insidious frost, its parched grains rubbing
At crannies, moved on our skin.
Our fingers died. Not the warmth
Of all my eight wide summers could keep me smiling.
The circle of the popping stove fell still
And we were early sped through the hurrying dark.

I ran through the bitterness on legs
That might have been brittle, my breath
Solid, grasping at stabs of bleak
Pain to gasp on. Winter branched in me, ice cracked
In my bleeding. When I fell through the teeth
Of the cold at my haven door I could not see

For locked tears, I could not feel the spent
Plenty of flames banked at the range.
Nor my father's hands as they roughed the blue
Of my knees. But I knew what he meant
With the love of his rueful laugh, and my true
World unfroze in a flood of happy crying,
As hot on my cheek as the sting of this present

Frost. I have stood too long in the orderly
Cold of the garden. I would not have again the death
Of that day come unasked as the comfortless dusk
Past the stakes of my fences. Yet these are my
Ghosts, they do not need to ask
For housing when the early frost comes down.
I take them in, all, to the settled warmth.

MIDWINTER

A grey, flat sky and a flat land, squeezing
The eye of the north. Great blows of snow
Swing on a blind wind as the staggering
Morning lurches itself half alive. A beast

Could not stand alive now. What sparrows flew
Flocks deep long ago lie soft in their feathery dust,

Their frail twigs splintered as ice. Furrows
Are nailed to the ground by winter's iron
And lie, emptied of seeding. A desperate noise
Is lost somewhere in the width of the cold.
Houses lean to the violence and gasp, holding on.
A small house shoulders lower, grips firmly its hold

On whatever safety the rigid season offers,
So that its man, stung loud awake by treachery
Of the year, runs to make the small flames burn
In the dead wood of his hearth, turns his wet eye
Aghast at the rolling window. He hears
With pain his dry blood rustle, with a little groan.

A FEBRUARY MORNING

This February morning, walking early to work
Across the frost-hung fields where the mild cattle
Stand wreathed in their own breath, I watch smooth
Starlings, loud handfuls of shot silk,
And hear my steps echo on the iron rime of the time.

Just as they echoed so sharply time out of mind ago
In my own country's cold
On the Dowlais moors at the dark of night
With one fierce unnatural star
Alone in the sky's arch.
Along the uncertain edge of the hanging mountain
The wild ponies limped and trembled,
Ice chiming like bells
In the long hair of their flanks. My footsteps,
Picked clean out of the cold and country air,
Hung their thin images on the ear's sharpness
For miles along the road
With never a near light nor comfortable sound.

But gently, and from no apparent direction,
The voice of a singing woman used the air,
Unhurried, passionate, clear, a voice of grief
Made quite impersonal by the night and hour.

For full five minutes' space along that mountain,
Not loudly nor ever fading away,
A full voice sang
Of such inhuman longing that I no more
Can say which was the song or which the fiery star.
One or the other lit the hollow road
That lay behind my clipped and winter steps
Time out of mind ago, in Wales.

This frosty morning, across the February fields
The militant bush of the sun in tawny splendour
Has not extinguished it, that song or star.

Vernon Scannell

Author's Introduction

It is difficult for anyone to write or speak honestly about his own poetry without seeming pompous, self-inflatory, disingenuous or over-earnest; to hear a mediocre writer of disposable verses droning on about his early work, influences and ambitions, treating his own stuff with something like the solemnity that most academic critics show before the texts of the undisputed heavyweight champions of the past, can be painfully embarrassing, so I hope to avoid this kind of nutty self-aggrandizement or the equally embarrassing tone of phoney self-deprecation by talking about poetry in general or the work of the poets I admire and only by implication nod towards my own intentions and aspirations.

The poetry that you enjoy reading and perhaps trying to write depends on the kind of person you are. If this remark seems obvious beyond the point of banality we might reflect that most critics and teachers of English Literature, at whatever level, work on the contrary assumption that the reader, whatever his temperamental predispositions, needs, prejudices, environment, intellect and education, is – or should be – equally responsive to all kinds of poetry, to Spenser as to Blake for instance, or to Pope as to Hopkins. Of course it is a fact that the wider the reader's taste the luckier he is, but most of us have a natural bias towards certain kinds of poetry just as we have a taste for certain kinds of food and drink (though preferences may change with changing circumstances) and these predilections are determined by social, biological and psychological factors over which we have no control.

Outside poetry my interest and sympathy are gained by whatever breathes, moves, suffers and delights, by whatever lives, and I am much less concerned with inanimate things. Technological marvels, abstract sculpture and painting, objects – natural or manufactured – however beautiful they may be to others hold comparatively little appeal for me. The nearest I come to taking an interest in anything scientific is some desultory reading in psychology and anthropology, both of which, of course, are directly concerned with human life. Not surprisingly, the kind of poetry that grips me is that which is firmly rooted in the living soil of recognizable human experience. I am well aware that this is a limiting and probably naive stance and, further, I am frequently shaken by finding myself moved and excited by poetry I would not have expected to appeal to me – by Wallace Stevens, for example, who has said, 'Life is not people and scene but thought and feeling' – but, in the main, it is the poetry of passion, of love, fear, hate, longing, wit, tenderness, violence and despair, the poetry which springs from the ground of common experience and contains the ambiguities and ironies that life itself contains, that offers me most nourishment, and writing of this kind is, of course, in the mainstream of English poetry from Chaucer, through the great Elizabethans and Jacobeans, on to Cowper, Crabbe, Wordsworth and Browning, to Hardy, Edward Thomas and W. H. Auden.

Very broadly speaking, there are three main kinds of poetry being written today in England: there is the pop and public poetry of protest, written for the voice rather than the page (on which, if it gets there, it generally looks pretty thin), work which is more closely related either to the entertainment world or the political soapbox rather than to any respectable literary ancestry; there is the mainstream, earth-rooted poetry I have mentioned and, finally, the neo-academic, attenuated and bloodless writing largely inspired by the American Black Mountain poets. These categories overlap a good deal, but in their extreme forms I have little time for the first and third, the first because, far from using language poetically (that is with maximum precision) it slops out the stock epithets, phrases and images of the ad man and pop lyricist and sets out to elicit the same stock responses; the third because it derives from what could be called the autotelic heresy, the view that maintains that it is impertinent to ask what a poem is *about*: a poem is not about anything, it simply exists, an autonomous verbal structure referring to nothing beyond itself. The trouble with this theory is that it does contain particles of truth but to ask what a poem is about seems to me a perfectly valid question though I concede that the answer, unless it is a reading of the poem, can be no more than partial and most certainly cannot replace the poem itself.

MASTERING THE CRAFT

To make the big time you must learn
The basic moves: left jab and hook,
The fast one-two, right-cross; the block
And counter-punch; the way to turn
Opponents on the ropes; the feint
To head or body; uppercut;
To move inside the swing and set
Your man up for the kill. But don't
Think that this is all; a mere
Beginning only. It is through
Fighting often you will grow
Accomplished in manoeuvres more
Subtle than the text-books know:
How to change your style to meet
The unexpected move that might
Leave you open to the blow
That puts the lights out for the night.

The same with poets: they must train,
Practise metre's footwork, learn
The old iambic left and right,
To change the pace and how to hold
The big punch till the proper time,
Jab away with accurate rhyme;
Adapt the style or be knocked cold.
But first the groundwork must be done.
Those poets who have never learnt
The first moves of the game, they can't
Hope to win.
                    Yet here comes one,
No style at all, untrained and fat,
Who still contrives to knock you flat.

NETTLES

My son aged three fell in the nettle bed.
'Bed' seemed a curious name for those green spears,
That regiment of spite behind the shed:

It was no place for rest. With sobs and tears
The boy came seeking comfort and I saw
White blisters beaded on his tender skin.
We soothed him till his pain was not so raw.
At last he offered us a watery grin,
And then I took my billhook, honed the blade
And went outside and slashed in fury with it
Till not a nettle in that fierce parade
Stood upright anymore. And then I lit
A funeral pyre to burn the fallen dead,
But in two weeks the busy sun and rain
Had called up tall recruits behind the shed:
My son would often feel sharp wounds again.

HORROR FILM

When he was nine years old he went
With pennies for the corpse's eyes.
He made the perilous descent
To cobwebbed cellar, heard the cries
Of dainty ladies making their
Involuntary gifts of blood.
A creature slunk towards its lair;
A strangled cat clawed at the mud;
A body in a coffin lay,
Soft conker in its satin case;
The candle flame was blown away,
But not before he saw the face
Staring through the dusty glass,
The fanged and slavering jaws agape,
The matted hair like withered grass,
That could not quite conceal the shape
Of almost human features, hide
The desperate appeal that cried
From self-accusing, frightened eyes.
The boy's own eyes were also wide
But not with fear; he recognized
Beneath the piteous brute disguise
The need for what might humanize:
The welcome or embrace that can
Change lonely monster into Man.

INCENDIARY

That one small boy with a face like pallid cheese
And burnt-out little eyes could make a blaze
As brazen, fierce and huge, as red and gold
And zany yellow as the one that spoiled
Three thousand guineas' worth of property
And crops at Godwin's Farm on Saturday
Is frightening – as fact and metaphor:
An ordinary match intended for
The lighting of a pipe or kitchen fire
Misused may set a whole menagerie
Of flame-fanged tigers roaring hungrily.
And frightening, too, that one small boy should set
The sky on fire and choke the stars to heat
Such skinny limbs and such a little heart
Which would have been content with one warm kiss
Had there been anyone to offer this.

AUTOBIOGRAPHICAL NOTE

Beeston, the place, near Nottingham:
We lived there for three years or so.
Each Saturday at two-o'clock
We queued up for the matinée,
All the kids for streets around
With snotty noses, giant caps,
Cut down coats and heavy boots,
The natural enemies of cops
And schoolteachers. Profane and hoarse
We scrambled, yelled and fought until
The Picture Palace opened up
And we, like Hamelin children, forced
Our bony way into the hall.
That much is easy to recall;
Also the reek of chewing-gum,
Gob-stoppers and liquorice,
But of the flickering myths themselves
Not much remains. The hero was
A milky wide-brimmed hat, a shape
Astride the arched white stallion;
The villain's horse and hat were black.
Disbelief did not exist

And laundered virtue always won
With quicker gun and harder fist,
And all of us applauded it.
Yet I remember moments when
In solitude I'd find myself
Brooding on the sooty man,
The bristling villain, who could move
Imagination in a way
The well-shaved hero never could,
And even warm the nervous heart
With something oddly close to love.

AUTUMN

It is the football season once more
And the back pages of the Sunday papers
Again show the blurred anguish of goalkeepers.

In Maida Vale, Golders Green and Hampstead
Lamps ripen early in the surprising dusk;
They are furred like stale rinds with a fuzz of mist.

The pavements of Kensington are greasy;
The wind smells of burnt porridge in Bayswater,
And the leaves are mushed to silence in the gutter.

The big hotel like an anchored liner
Rides near the park; lit windows hammer the sky.
Like the slow swish of surf the tyres of taxis sigh.

On Ealing Broadway the cinema glows
Warm behind glass while mellow the church clock chimes
As the waiting girls stir in their delicate chains.

Their eyes are polished by the wind,
But the gleam is dumb, empty of joy or anger.
Though the lovers are long in coming the girls still linger.

We are nearing the end of the year.
Under the sombre sleeve the blood ticks faster
And in the dark ear of Autumn quick voices whisper.

It is a time of year that's to my taste,
Full of spiced rumours, sharp and velutinous flavours,
Dim with the mist that softens the cruel surfaces,
Makes mirrors vague. It is the mist that I most favour.

END OF A SEASON

The nights are drawing in; the daylight dies
With more dispatch each evening;
Traffic draws lit beads
Across the bridge's abacus.
Below, black waters jitter in a breeze.
The air is not yet cold
But woven in its woof of various blues,
Whiffs of petrol and cremated flowers,
A cunning thread runs through,
A thin premonitory chill.
The parks are closed. Lights beckon from the bars.
The sporting news has put on heavier dress.
It is not autumn yet
Though summer will not fill
Attentive hearts again with its warm yes.

Far from the city, too, the dark surprises:
Oak and sycamore hunch
Under their loads of leaves;
Plump apples fall; the night devises
Frail webs to vein the sleek skin of the plums.
The scent of stars is cold.
The wheel-ruts stumble in the lane, are dry and hard.
Night is a nest for the unhatched cries of owls;
As deep mines clench their gold
Night locks up autumn's voices in
The vaults of silence. Hedges are still shawled
With traveller's joy; yet windows of the inn
Rehearse a winter welcome.
Though tomorrow may be fine
Soon it will yield to night's swift drawing in.

The athletes of light evenings hibernate;
Their whites are folded round
Green stains; the night
Reminds with its old merchandise –
Those summer remnants on its highest boughs –

That our late dancing days
Are doomed if not already under ground.
The playground gates are chained; the swings hang still,
The lovers have come down
From their deciduous hill;
Others may climb again, but they will not.
And yet the heart resumes its weightier burden
With small reluctance; fares
Towards Fall, and then beyond
To winter with whom none can fool or bargain.

OLD MAN'S SONG

The baby bawling, being sick,
The spotty girl with hockey-stick
Who dreams of pink blancmange and pie,
Might not be
Ideally
Happy but I know they are
Far better off than I.

I watch the warm limbs jolly by,
Feel neither grand nor fatherly:
I don't long
For those strong
Bodies but how achingly
I desire desire.

Friday night boys as bold as Bass
Release their lusts like poison gas
In punching yells or foggy songs;
That in the end
They will descend
To my cellar does not ease
This thorny hat of wrongs.

The autumn leaves romantically
Die gay and suicidally
And night is hurt by the owl's cry;
The still sleeper
Sleeps deeper
Whom no alarming clock will shock:
He's better off than I.

Cat in the night clawing silence
Howling lust that needs no licence
Makes me want to want to die;
Even though
They don't know
Dogs and bitches bogged in ditches
Are far better off than I.

HERE AND HUMAN

In the warm room, cushioned by comfort,
Idle at fireside, shawled in lamplight,
I know the cold winter night, but only
As a far intimation, like a memory
Of a dead distress whose ghost has grown genial.

The disc, glossy black as a conjurer's hat,
Revolves. Music is unwound: woodwind,
Strings, a tenor voice singing in a tongue
I do not comprehend or have need to –
'The instrument of egoism mastered by art' –

For what I listen to is unequivocal:
A distillation of romantic love,
Passion outsoaring speech. I understand
And, understanding, I rejoice in my condition:
This sweet accident of being here and human.

Later, as I lie in the dark, the echoes
Recede, the blind cat of sleep purrs close
But does not curl. Beyond the window
The hill is hunched under his grey cape
Like a watchman. I cannot hear his breathing.

Silence is a starless sky on the ceiling
Till shock slashes, stillness is gashed
By a dazzle of noise chilling the air
Like lightning. It is an animal screech,
Raucous, clawing: surely the language of terror.

But I misread it, deceived. It is the sound
Of passionate love, a vixen's mating call.

It lingers hurtful, a stink in the ear,
But soon it begins to fade. I breathe deep,
Feeling the startled fur settle and smooth. Then I sleep.

JAILBIRD

His plumage is dun,
Talons long but blunt.
His appetite is indiscriminate.
He has no mate and sleeps alone
In a high nest built of brick and steel.
He sings at night
A long song, sad and silent.
He cannot fly.

PICNIC ON THE LAWN

Their dresses were splashed on the green
Like big petals; polished spoons shone
And tinkered with cup and saucer.
Three women sat there together.

They were young, but no longer girls.
Above them the soft green applause
Of leaves acknowledged their laughter.
Their voices moved at a saunter.

Small children were playing nearby;
A swing hung from an apple tree
And there was a sand pit for digging.
Two of the picnicking women

Were mothers. The third was not.
She had once had a husband, but
He had gone to play the lover
With a new lead in a different theatre.

One of the mothers said, 'Have you
Cherished a dream, a fantasy
You know is impossible; a childish
Longing to do something wildly

'Out of character? I'll tell you mine.
I would like to drive alone
In a powerful sports car, wearing
A headscarf and dark glasses, looking

'Sexy and mysterious and rich.'
The second mother smiled: 'I wish
I could ride through an autumn morning
On a chestnut mare, cool wind blowing

'The jet black hair I never had
Like smoke streaming from my head,
In summer swoop on a switchback sea
Surf-riding in a black bikini.'

She then turned to the childless one:
'And you? You're free to make dreams true.
You have no need of fantasies
Like us domestic prisoners.'

A pause, and then the answer came:
'I also have a hopeless dream:
Tea on the lawn in a sunny garden,
Listening to the voices of my children.'

THE JEALOUS WIFE

Like a private eye she searches
For clues through diaries and papers;
Examines his clothing for the guilty stains
Of crimson lipstick, wicked wine,
Or something biological.
And when no act of sensual
Crime can be at length surmised
She is most puzzled and surprised
To be assailed by disappointment
Not relief. Her steel intent
Is never to betray to him
The blonde and naked thoughts within
The purple bedroom of her mind,
But her resolve can never stand
The pressure of the need to know:
'Where?' she says and 'When?' and 'Who?'

'What time?' 'What day?' The question-marks
Like powerful iron grappling hooks
Drag him to her fantasy.
And then he cannot fail to see
Within the harem of her skull
The lovely wickednesses loll.
Thus, at night, they softly creep,
Tap at the darkened panes of sleep;
Then, white and tender, glide inside
His dream on whose delightful slope
At last her fears are justified.

WIFE KILLER

He killed his wife at night.
He had tried once or twice in the daylight
But she refused to die.

In darkness the deed was done,
Not crudely with a hammer-hard gun
Or strangler's black kid gloves on.

She just ceased being alive,
Not there to interfere or connive,
Linger, leave or arrive.

It seemed almost as though
Her death was quite normal and no
Clue to his part would show.

So then, with impunity,
He called up that buttocky beauty
He had so long longed to see

All covering gone: the double
Joggle of warm weighty bubbles
Was sweet delirious trouble.

And all night, all night he enjoyed her;
Such sport in her smooth dimpled water;
Then daylight came like a warder.

And he rose and went down to the larder
Where the mouse-trap again had caught a
Piece of stale gorgonzola.

His wife wore her large woollen feet.
She said that he was late
And asked what he wanted to eat,

But said nothing about the murder –
And who, after all, could have told her?
He said that he fancied a kipper.

LEGS

Of well-fed babies activate
Digestive juices, yet I'm no cannibal.
It is my metaphysical teeth that wait
Impatiently to prove these goodies edible.
The pink or creamy bonelessness, as soft
As dough or mashed potato, does not show
A hint of how each pair of limbs will grow.
Schoolboys' are badged with scabs and starred with scars,
Their sisters' in white ankle socks possess
No calves as yet. They will, and when they do
Another kind of hunger will distress
Quite painfully, but pleasurably too.
Those lovely double stalks of girls give me
So much delight: the brown expensive ones,
Like fine twin creatures of rare pedigree,
Seem independent of their owners, so
Much themselves are they. Even the plain
Or downright ugly, the veined and cruelly blotched
That look like marble badly stained, I've watched
With pity and revulsion, yet something more –
A wonder at the variousness of things
Which share a name: the podgy oatmeal knees
Beneath the kilt, the muscled double weapons above boots,
Eloquence of dancers', suffering of chars',
The wiry goatish, the long and smooth as milk—
The joy when these embrace like arms and cling!
O human legs, whose strangenesses I sing,
You more than please, though pleasure you have brought me,
And there are often times when you transport me.

GUNPOWDER PLOT

For days these curious cardboard buds have lain
In brightly coloured boxes. Soon the night
Will come. We pray there'll be no rain
To make these magic orchids flame less bright.

Now in the garden's darkness they begin
To flower: the frenzied whizz of Catherine-wheel
Puts forth its fiery petals and the thin
Rocket soars to burst upon the steel

Bulwark of a cloud. And then the guy,
Absurdly human phoenix, is again
Gulped by greedy flames: the harvest sky
Is flecked with threshed and golden grain.

'Uncle! A cannon! Watch me as I light it!'
The women, helter-skelter, squealing high,
Retreat; the paper fuse is quickly lit,
A cat-like hiss and spit of fire, a sly

Falter, then the air is shocked with blast.
The cannon bangs, and in my nostrils drifts
A bitter scent that brings the lurking past
Lurching to my side. The present shifts,

Allows a ten-year memory to walk
Unhindered now; and so I'm forced to hear
The banshee howl of mortar and the talk
Of men who died; am forced to taste my fear.

I listen for a moment to the guns,
The torn earth's grunts, recalling how I prayed.
The past retreats. I hear a corpse's sons:
'Who's scared of bangers?' 'Uncle! John's afraid!'

BATTLEFIELDS

Tonight in the pub I talked with Ernie Jones
Who served with the Somersets in Normandy,
And we remembered how our fathers told
The sad and muddy legends of their war,

And how, as youngsters, we would grin and say:
'The old man's on his favourite topic now,
He never tires of telling us the tale.'
We are the old men now, our turn has come.
The names have changed – Tobruk and Alamein,
Arnhem, the Falaise Gap and Caen Canal
Displace the Dardanelles, Gallipoli,
Vimy Ridge, the Somme – but little else.
Our children do not want to hear about
The days when we were young and, sometimes, brave,
And who can blame them? Certainly not us.
We drank a last half pint and said goodnight.
And now, at home, the family is in bed,
The kitchen table littered with crashed planes;
A tank is tilted on its side, one track
Has been blown off; behind the butter-dish
Two Gunners kneel, whose gun has disappeared;
A Grenadier with busby and red coat
Mounts guard before a half a pound of cheese.
Some infantry with bayonets fixed begin
A slow advance towards the table edge.
Conscripted from another time and place
A wild Apache waves his tomahawk.
It's all a game. Upstairs, my youngest son
Roars like a little Stuka as he dives
Through dream, banks steep, then cuts his engine out,
Levels, re-enters the armistice of sleep.

REMEMBRANCE DAY

Apposite blood red the blobs
Of artificial poppies count
Our annual dead.
The garment of lament is worn
Threadbare and each medal hangs
Heavy its shameful head.

Bugles make their sad assault
Upon the heart and spine and throat
Ordering regret.
The names evoked are usual:
Passchendaele, Bapaume and Loos –
Our cheeks are wet.

And fumbling for the right response
We summon names more personal:
Nobby, Frank and Ted.
But wormy years have eaten their
Identities and none can mourn
These artificial dead.

And when a true emotion strikes
It strikes a crude, unsanctioned blow
Which brings a harsher chill
To hearts that know that they grow old
And must grow older yet before
That terrible Until.

WALKING WOUNDED

A mammoth morning moved grey flanks and groaned.
In the rusty hedges pale rags of mist hung;
The gruel of mud and leaves in the mauled lane
Smelled sweet, like blood. Birds had died or flown,
Their green and silent attics sprouting now
With branches of leafed steel, hiding round eyes
And ripe grenades ready to drop and burst.
In the ditch at the cross-roads the fallen rider lay
Hugging his dead machine and did not stir
At crunch of mortar, tantrum of a Bren
Answering a Spandau's manic jabber.
Then into sight the ambulances came,
Stumbling and churning past the broken farm,
The amputated sign-post and smashed trees,
Slow wagonloads of bandaged cries, square trucks
That rolled on ominous wheels, vehicles
Made mythopoeic by their mortal freight
And crimson crosses on the dirty white.
This grave procession passed, though, for a while,
The grinding of their engines could be heard,
A dark noise on the pallor of the morning,
Dark as dried blood; and then it faded, died.
The road was empty, but it seemed to wait –
Like a stage which knows the cast is in the wings –
Wait for a different traffic to appear.
The mist still hung in snags from dripping thorns;
Absent-minded guns still sighed and thumped.

And then they came, the walking wounded,
Straggling the road like convicts loosely chained,
Dragging at ankles exhaustion and despair.
Their heads were weighted down by last night's lead,
And eyes still drank the dark. They trailed the night
Along the morning road. Some limped on sticks;
Others wore rough dressings, splints and slings;
A few had turbanned heads, the dirty cloth
Brown-badged with blood. A humble brotherhood,
Not one was suffering from a lethal hurt,
They were not magnified by noble wounds,
There was no splendour in that company.
And yet, remembering after eighteen years,
In the heart's throat a sour sadness stirs;
Imagination pauses and returns
To see them walking still, but multiplied
In thousands now. And when heroic corpses
Turn slowly in their decorated sleep
And every ambulance has disappeared
The walking wounded still trudge down that lane,
And when recalled they must bear arms again.

UNCLE EDWARD'S AFFLICTION

Uncle Edward was colour-blind;
We grew accustomed to the fact.
When he asked someone to hand him
The green book from the window-seat
And we observed its bright red cover
Either apathy or tact
Stifled comment. We passed it over.
Much later, I began to wonder
What curious world he wandered in,
Down streets where pea-green pillar-boxes
Grinned at a fire-engine as green;
How Uncle Edward's sky at dawn
And sunset flooded marshy green.
Did he ken John Peel with his coat so green
And Robin Hood in Lincoln red?
On country walks avoid being stung
By nettles hot as a witch's tongue?
What meals he savoured with his eyes:
Green strawberries and fresh red peas,

Green beef and greener burgundy.
All unscientific, so it seems:
His world was not at all like that,
So those who claim to know have said.
Yet, I believe, in war-smashed France
He must have crawled from neutral mud
To lie in pastures dark and red
And seen, appalled, on every blade
The rain of innocent green blood.

EPITHETS OF WAR – I: AUGUST 1914

The bronze sun blew a long and shimmering call
Over the waves of Brighton and Southend,
Over slapped and patted pyramids of sand,
Paper Union Jacks and cockle stalls;
A pierrot aimed his banjo at the gulls;
Small spades dug trenches to let the channel in
As nimble donkeys followed their huge heads
And charged. In the navy sky the loud white birds
Lolled on no wind, then, swinging breathless, skimmed
The somersaulting waves; a military band
Thumped and brayed, brass pump of sentiment;
And far from the beach, inland, lace curtains stirred,
A girl played Chopin while her sister pored
Over her careful sewing; faint green scent
Of grass was sharpened by a gleam of mint,
And, farther off, in London, horses pulled
Their rumbling drays and vans along the Strand
Or trundled down High Holborn and beyond
The Stadium Club, where, in the wounded world
Of five years later, Georges Carpentier felled
Bulldog Joe Beckett in a single round.
And all is history; its pages smell
Faintly of camphor and dead pimpernel
Coffined in leaves, and something of the sand
And salt of holiday. But dead. The end
Of something never to be lived again.

EPITHETS OF WAR – III: CASUALTIES

They were printed daily in the newspapers.
A woman in Nottingham went mad reading them;
She drowned herself in the Trent.
Her name was not included in the casualty lists.

She was mother of two million sons.
At night a frail voice would quaver,
Cry from its bed of mud:
'Stretcher-bearers! Stretcher-bearers!' She could not go.

She could not bear it. Her mind broke.
Barbed-wire scrawled illiterate history
Over the black dough of Belgian fields,
Was punctuated by anatomies.

In Trafalgar Square an English lady
Distributed white feathers among civilians.
Children with sad moustaches and puttee'd calves
Prepared to be translated.

The crazed mother heard them at night
Crying as hot stars exploded
And the earth's belly shook and rumbled
With giant eructations.

The ambulances lurched through the mire in the brain;
Uniformed surgeons in crimson aprons
Laboured at irreparable bodies;
Dawn bristled on their skullish jaws.

And two million of an innocent generation,
Orphaned by a doomed, demented mother,
Unlearned an axiom: they discovered
Only the lucky few meet death once only.

THE BOMBING OF THE CAFE DE PARIS 1941

Snakehips, the bandleader, wore a gallant grin,
A clip of white cartridges; he and the boys

Tapped natty polished toes to keep the time
Of tango, quickstep, foxtrot, blues and swing;
The basement of the place was deep and safe,
No other-ranks or bombs would be let in.

A boy in Air Force blue danced with his mother;
A sub-lieutenant stroked his girl's silk knee;
Caressing lights lay soft on hair and flesh,
Bright on badges, deep in polished leather.
A major of The Black Watch called for Scotch
And winked at his admiring younger brother.

Oh Johnny, Oh Johnny, how you can love,
That was the song they liked. They could forget
That loving wasn't all that he must do:
Oh Johnny, Oh Johnny, heavens above –
And in the hidden heavens the siren's wailing
Mourned over London and the shattered dove.

But no one there could hear. The music gushed
And wine corks popped like children's wooden guns.
No warning when the bomb came bursting in,
Huge knuckle-dustered fist that struck and crushed
Furniture of wood and flesh; the bang's
Enormous shadow paled; the place was hushed.

Some light remained, and from the ceiling came
Floating down a fine cosmetic dust
That settled softly on the hair and skin
Of the sailor's girl, who, wholly without shame,
Sprawled in ripped clothes, one precious stocking
gone
And with it half her leg. No one would blame

Her carelessness for once, and if they did
She would not care. The sailor lay beneath
Dark flood of fallen curtain, quiet and still,
As if he rested on the ocean bed.
The airman's mother sat upon the floor,
Crooned comfort to her child's deaf cradled head.

Snakehips had put away his grin forever.
Music might return, but he would not.
The kilted major found another drink

Then carried out his brother, like an order,
Joining the stunned survivors in the street,
Sick from their meeting with the dark marauder.

While, down below, a woman lay and saw
A man approaching through the powdery gloom;
She could not move trapped limbs. 'Rescue!' she
thought
As by her side he knelt upon the floor,
Reached out to finger at her neck and take
Her string of pearls in one triumphant paw.

Outside, the sirens once again composed
A mocking dirge above the crouching town;
Along the blackened streets on nervous wheels
The blinkered ambulances gently nosed,
Ferrying cool instruments of mercy.
An incident of war was almost closed.

Anthony Thwaite

Author's Introduction

What many of these poems have in common is that they look at some particular object or survival from the past. In a real and literal sense, our world is made up of countless layers of the past: we exist through what has gone before. A grave, a ruin, an ancient Greek coin picked up from the ground, a few written words – these things link us to our ancestors. And we too, in our turn, will be ancestors. The past, the present and the future are unendingly joined.

'The Barrow.' A Bronze Age burial mound in Gloucestershire, which was dug and robbed, like so many of these barrows, probably in the eighteenth or nineteenth century.

'At Dunkeswell Abbey.' The ruins of Dunkeswell Abbey are on the borders of Devon and Somerset. During the sixteenth-century Reformation, its monks were driven out and its buildings began to be pulled down. Most monastic sites had ponds for breeding fish, so that there was a constant supply of fresh food.

'At Dunwich.' Dunwich (pronounced Dunnitch) is now a tiny hamlet on the coast of Suffolk, but it was a large and flourishing town in the Middle Ages, with many churches – probably more than fifteen, in fact. The North Sea has gradually eaten into the cliffs and destroyed the place.

'Cleaning a Coin.' For two years (1965–67) I lived in Benghazi, in eastern Libya. This part of North Africa was colonized by the Greeks, beginning in the sixth century B.C. I often found coins in the ruins of these Greek colonial settlements. Putting an encrusted ancient coin in a cup of vinegar diluted with water is an amateurish way of cleaning it; a proper archaeologist with a laboratory would use a method known as electrolysis. Really, you are *not* meant to use a knife to scrape at it, as this may damage the coin.

'Ali Ben Shufti.' At the ancient Greek colonial city of Ptolemais (now Tolmeita) in Libya, I came across a man who made a living by selling antiquities he had found to tourists or foreign archaeologists. He was not really called Ali Ben Shufti – *shufti* is a crude way, picked up by the British army in the Middle East, of saying 'look!' in Arabic. The first two lines of the poem are meant to be the man himself speaking in his broken English: the rest is what I imagine he is thinking to himself. 'The disturbances' of the museum labels are those of the Second World War, in which Libya was a battleground, fought over by the Germans, the Italians and the British. The 'college bodysnatchers' is a rude way of describing the visiting archaeologists. Amr Ibn el-As was the great Arab general who, in the seventh century A.D., waged a lightning military campaign along the North African coast, subduing it all to the Muslim faith of the Arabs. A piastre is (or was) about 1p.

'Monologue in the Valley of the Kings.' Imagine some Pharaoh, lying deep in his magnificent tomb in the Valley of the Kings in Upper Egypt (where Tutankhamen, among others, was discovered), talking to the modern archaeologist who is trying to find him. But it is also, I think, a poem about the buried or hidden self – that secret part of you you can never reveal, even to those closest to you.

'Arabic Script.' An Englishman I knew in Libya mockingly said that Arabic writing looked as if a spider had been crawling through a blot of ink: squiggles and dots and dashes. The dots and dashes are known by linguists as *diacritical* signs, and they indicate accents on vowels. Sidi Kreibish is the old Muslim cemetery in Benghazi, built on top of the Hellenistic city: the gravestones there carry inscriptions in the style of Arabic writing known as Kufic – very firm, angular and strong. The armies of Amr Ibn el-As (see 'Ali Ben Shufti') passed this way, conquering the feeble Graeco-Roman settlers ('flaccid colonials'). The crescent of Islam would be on their battle standards.

'Entry.' The few lines quoted at the top are taken from an eighteenth-century parish register of births and deaths. 'Moses Ozier' must have been the invention of the verger who wrote down the entry, after having first christened the dying baby – the illegitimate child of an insane pauper woman who, without any home of her own, gave birth among the rushes and reeds belonging to a local landowner.

'Inscriptions.' Three kinds of inscription are brought together: on a lavatory door, an anarchist slogan painted up on a wall, and the pious words carved on Victorian gravestones. Whatever wild ideas we have about sex or politics, we all die sooner or later.

'Switzerland.' I saw a small military band practising in a field at St Gallen in Switzerland. The Swiss, with a highly trained part-time army, have managed to keep out of wars for centuries.

'Soldiers Plundering a Village.' On one day I happened to see some photographs of atrocities in Vietnam and a book of pictures by seventeenth-century Netherlandish *genre* painters (that is, painters of everyday life). 'Soldiers Plundering a Village' is the actual title of a painting by the minor artist Pieter Snayers: the quoted comments are by a modern art-historian about him. The details described in the poem come from this painting.

'At Asqefar.' A place about 40 miles north-east of Benghazi, where I saw the German helmet and the ancient cave on the walls of which are painted scenes concerned with Ulysses and the return from Troy, probably made in the first or second century A.D. There was fierce fighting in this area during the North African campaigns of the Second World War.

'Worm Within.' My wife and I brought back from holiday in Sicily a rough wooden doll of a traditional peasant kind – though nowadays these things are produced in vast quantities specially for tourists like ourselves. Back in England, it turned out to contain something that terrifies any house-owner. (Incidentally, when this poem was first published, in the *Observer*, I received an interested letter from Rentokil a few days later . . .)

'Lesson.' I have never been in a slaughterhouse, but read in a book an account of the way in which young animals are kept quiet in such places by being led to their deaths by older animals – the so-called 'Judas beasts'. The poem is *not* an attack on teachers.

'The Foresters Arms.' A pub with this name, glimpsed from a train while travelling through a hideous industrialized part of the Midlands.

'Two Faces.' When I was in my teens, I wanted to look older and more experienced; but as one gets *really* older . . . (This poem, which was first published in the *New York Times*, also resulted in a letter – this time from a lady living in the state of Maine, who said she thought I must have a most interesting face, and offered to paint my portrait for half her usual fee. She seems to have missed the point of the poem.)

'Called For.' Collecting my seventeen-year-old daughter from a pop concert in Norwich. In 1957, just before she was born, I wrote a poem called 'To my Unborn Child', which was published in my first book and which has appeared in a few anthologies. To a parent, there's something poignant, as well as cheerful, about one's children growing up.

THE BARROW

In this high field strewn with stones
I walk by a green mound,
Its edges sheared by the plough.
Crumbs of animal bone
Lie smashed and scattered round
Under the clover leaves
And slivers of flint seem to grow
Like white leaves among green.
In the wind, the chestnut heaves
Where a man's grave has been.

Whatever the barrow held
Once, has been taken away:
A hollow of nettles and dock
Lies at the centre, filled
With rain from a sky so grey
It reflects nothing at all.
I poke in the crumbled rock
For something they left behind
But after that funeral
There is nothing at all to find.

On the map in front of me
The gothic letters pick out
Dozens of tombs like this,
Breached, plundered, left empty,
No fragments littered about
Of a dead and buried race
In the margins of histories.
No fragments: these splintered bones
Construct no human face,
These stones are simply stones.

In museums their urns lie
Behind glass, and their shaped flints
Are labelled like butterflies.
All that they did was die,
And all that has happened since
Means nothing to this place.

Above long clouds, the skies
Turn to a brilliant red
And show in the water's face
One living, and not these dead.

AT DUNKESWELL ABBEY

Below the ford, the stream in flood
Rises and laps the leaf-choked wood
And fallen branches trap thick mud.
Pebbles are swept like slingstones down
Runnels and channels sliced through stone
And in the hollows sink and drown.

On either side broad ramparts hold
The water back from copse and field,
Where a dry earthbank seems to fold
Protectively a hollow space
Of pasture edged with stunted trees
In its inert and curved embrace.

Six hundred years ago, great pike
Grown old in this man-fashioned lake
Swam through its lily clusters like
Dream-presences below the mind.
Dark waters stirred where now I stand
Hearing the distant stream unwind.

The stillness here was made to last.
Whatever shapes survive exist
In some faint diagram of the past,
A sketch-map tentative as those
Robbed walls whose simulacrum lies
In patches summer droughts expose.

One wall still overtops the trees
Beyond the ford, but bramble grows
Round rotten stone. What energies
Persist are harnessed to the stream,
Violent in flood, not curbed or tame,
And hurtling without plan or aim.

AT DUNWICH

Fifteen churches lie here
Under the North Sea;
Forty-five years ago
The last went down the cliff.
You can see, at low tide,
A mound of masonry
Chewed like a damp bun.

In the village now (if you call
Dunwich a village now,
With a handful of houses, one street,
And a shack for Tizer and tea)
You can ask an old man
To show you the stuff they've found
On the beach when there's been a storm:

Knife-blades, buckles and rings,
Enough coins to fill an old sock,
Badges that men wore
When they'd been on pilgrimage,
Armfuls of broken pots.
People cut bread, paid cash,
Buttoned up against the cold.

Fifteen churches, and men
In thousands working at looms,
And wives brewing up stews
In great grey cooking pots.
I put out a hand and pull
A sherd from the cliff's jaws.
The sand trickles, then falls.

Nettles grow on the cliffs
In clumps as high as a house.
The houses have gone away.
Stand and look at the sea
Eating the land as it walks
Steadily treading the tops
Of fifteen churches' spires.

CLEANING A COIN

The green encrusted lump
Stews in its vinegar.
I peck with a pocket knife
At accretions of shell and stone.
Sand flakes from the centre.

After three days of this
The alchemy takes over.
Through a mask of verdigris
A profile stares through,
Wild-haired and chapleted.

And there on the other side
A vestigial horse capers
Across an illegible
Inscription in Greek. I rinse
The tiny disc at the tap.

I keep it now on my desk
With the other beachcombings,
This rendering down of the last
Twenty-five centuries
To a scoured chip of bleached bronze.

ALI BEN SHUFTI

You want coins? Roman? Greek? Nice vase? Head of god,
goddess?
Look, shufti here, very cheap. Two piastres? You joke.

I poke among fallen stones, molehills, the spoil
Left by the archaeologists and carelessly sieved.
I am not above ferreting out a small piece
From the foreman's basket when his back is turned.
One or two of my choicer things were acquired
During what the museum labels call 'the disturbances
Of 1941': you may call it loot,
But I keep no records of who my vendors were –
Goatherds, Johnnies in berets, Neapolitan conscripts
Hot foot out of trouble, dropping a keepsake or two.
I know a good thing, I keep a quiet ear open when

The college bodysnatchers arrive from Chicago,
Florence, Oxford, discussing periods
And measuring everything. I've even done business with them:
You will find my anonymous presence in the excavation reports
When you get to 'Finds Locally Purchased'. Without a B.A. –
And unable to read or write – I can date and price
Any of this rubbish. Here, from my droll pantaloons
That sag in the seat, amusing you no end,
I fetch out Tanagra heads, blue Roman beads,
A Greek lamp, bronze from Byzantium,
A silver stater faced with the head of Zeus.
I know three dozen words of English, enough French
To settle a purchase, and enough Italian
To convince the austere *dottore* he's made a bargain.
As for the past, it means nothing to me but this:
A time when things were made to keep me alive.
You are the ones who go on about it: I survive
By scratching it out with my fingers. I make you laugh
By being obsequious, roguish, battered, in fact
What you like to think of as a typical Arab.
Well, Amr Ibn el-As passed this way
Some thirteen hundred years ago, and we stayed.
I pick over what he didn't smash, and you
Pay for the leavings. That is enough for me.
You take them away and put them on your shelves
And for fifty piastres I give you a past to belong to.

MONOLOGUE IN THE VALLEY OF THE KINGS

I have hidden something in the inner chamber
And sealed the lid of the sarcophagus
And levered a granite boulder against the door
And the debris has covered it so perfectly
That though you walk over it daily you never suspect.

Every day you sweat down that shaft, seeing on the walls
The paintings that convince you I am at home, living there.
But that is a blind alley, a false entrance
Flanked by a room with a few bits of junk
Nicely displayed, conventionally chosen.
The throne is quaint but commonplace, the jewels inferior,

The decorated panels not of the best period,
Though enough is there to satisfy curators.

But the inner chamber enshrines the true essence.
Do not be disappointed when I tell you
You will never find it: the authentic phoenix in gold,
The muslin soaked in herbs from recipes
No one remembers, the intricate ornaments,
And above all the copious literatures inscribed
On ivory and papyrus, the distilled wisdom
Of priests, physicians, poets and gods,
Ensuring my immortality. Though even if you found them
You would look in vain for the key, since all are in cipher
And the key is in my skull.

The key is in my skull. If you found your way
Into this chamber, you would find this last:
My skull. But first you would have to search the others,
My kinsfolk neatly parcelled, twenty-seven of them
Disintegrating in their various ways.
A woman from whose face the spices have pushed away
The delicate flaking skin: a man whose body
Seems dipped in clotted black tar, his head detached:
A hand broken through the cerements, protesting:
Mouths in rigid grins or soundless screams –
A catalogue of declensions.

How, then, do I survive? Gagged in my winding cloths,
The four brown roses withered on my chest
Leaving a purple stain, how am I different
In transcending these little circumstances?
Supposing that with uncustomary skill
You penetrated the chamber, granite, seals,
Dragged out the treasure gloatingly, distinguished
My twenty-seven sorry relatives,
Labelled them, swept and measured everything
Except this one sarcophagus, leaving that
Until the very end: supposing then
You lifted me out carefully under the arc-lamps,
Noting the gold fingernails, the unearthly smell
Of preservation – would you not tremble
At the thought of who this might be? So you would steady
Your hands a moment, like a man taking aim, and lift
The mask.

But this hypothesis is absurd. I have told you already
You will never find it. Daily you walk about
Over the rubble, peer down the long shaft
That leads nowhere, make your notations, add
Another appendix to your laborious work.
When you die, decently cremated, made proper
By the Registrar of Births and Deaths, given by *The Times*
Your two-inch obituary, I shall perhaps
Have a chance to talk with you. Until then, I hear
Your footsteps over my head as I lie and think
Of what I have hidden here, perfect and safe.

ARABIC SCRIPT

Like a spider through ink, someone says, mocking: see it
Blurred on the news-sheets or in neon lights
And it suggests an infinitely plastic, feminine
Syllabary, all the diacritical dots and dashes
Swimming together like a shoal of minnows,
Purposive yet wayward, a wavering measure
Danced over meaning, obscuring vowels and breath.
But at Sidi Kreibish, among the tombs,
Where skulls lodge in the cactus roots,
The pink claws breaking headstone, cornerstone,
Each fleshy tip thrusting to reach the light,
Each spine a hispid needle, you see the stern
Edge of the language, Kufic, like a scimitar
Curved in a lash, a flash of consonants
Such as swung out of Medina that day
On the long flog west, across ruins and flaccid colonials,
A swirl of black flags, white crescents, a language of swords.

ENTRY

Died, 1778*: Moses Ozier, son of a woman out of her mind,*
born in the ozier ground belonging to Mr Craft.

Christened with scripture, eponymously labelled,
You lie so small and shrunken in the verger's tall
Archaic writing. Born in the low water meadows
Down the end of lawns where you would be unlikely to walk
Supposing you'd ever got that far in life, no Pharaoh's daughter

Plucked you out of the bulrushes, for this was Yorkshire
And prophets had stopped being born. Your lunatic mother
Knelt in the rushes and squirmed in her brute pain,
Delivering you up to a damp punishing world
Where the ducks were better off, and the oziers wetly rustled
Sogged down in the marshland owned by Mr Craft.

It's sense to suppose you lasted a few days
And were buried, gratis, in an unmarked hole at the edge
Of the churchyard, the verger being scrupulous
And not wanting your skinny christened bundle of bones
To lie in unhallowed ground.

Poor tiny Moses,
Your white face is a blank, anonymous
Like other people's babies. Almost two hundred years
Since you briefly lay by the cold and placid river,
And nothing but nineteen words as memorial.

I hear you cry in the night at the garden's dark edge.

INSCRIPTIONS

Knickers Fisher has been at work again,
Using a compass point on the closet door,
But he's a miniaturist whose main concern
Is altogether different from the team
Exhibiting on the wall by the railway line:
SMASH THE STATE stands six feet high or more
In strong black paint where the track crosses the stream –
Opposites in the field of graphic design.

And in the middle scale are the stone slabs
Pecked out by masons dead these hundred years,
Gravestones along the passage to the town:
They make their claims too, with a different voice,
But still in hope and expectation. They
Exhort and yearn and stiffly mask the fears
Of men with large obsessions and small choice,
Burdened with flesh and law till judgement day.

SWITZERLAND

In a valley in Switzerland a brass band marches.
The dapper chalets twinkle in the sun
Among the meadows and the well-drilled larches
And watercourses where streams briskly run.

Bravely the little drums pretend their thunder
To far-off crags whose melting snow brings down
A rattle of small pebbles buried under
Drifts deeper than the church spire in the town.

The soldier-citizens of the canton practise
Before an audience of sheep and cows.
As for the real thing, the simple fact is
Each keeps a well-oiled rifle in his house.

Duchies and principalities have fathered
These drums and cornets under angrier skies,
Bucolic bellicosities which gathered
The Ruritanian airs of paradise

Into a clockwork joke envious Europe
Could laugh at, play in, patronize, ignore,
As, poised between the saddle and the stirrup,
The Switzer was acknowledged as a bore.

The peaceable kingdom rests on marks and dollars
Beside the lake at Zurich, lined with banks,
Far from the towns draped with insurgent colours
Whose dawn breaks with the grinding tread of tanks.

The Alpine avalanche holds back this summer
Its fragile tons, and watches from the height
The nimble piper and the strutting drummer
Putting the valley's herbivores to flight.

SOLDIERS PLUNDERING A VILLAGE

Down the mud road, between tall bending trees,
Men thickly move, then fan out one by one
Into the foreground. Far left, a soldier tries
Bashing a tame duck's head in with a stick,

While on a log his smeared companion
Sits idly by a heap of casual loot –
Jugs splashing over, snatched-up joints of meat.

Dead centre, a third man has spiked a fourth –
An evident civilian, with one boot
Half off, in flight, face white, lungs short of breath.
Out of a barn another soldier comes,
Gun at the ready, finding at his feet
One more old yokel, gone half mad with fear,
Tripped in his path, wild legs up in the air.

Roofs smashed, smoke rising, distant glow of fire,
A woman's thighs splayed open after rape
And lying there still: charred flecks caught in the air,
And caught for ever by a man from Antwerp
Whose style was 'crudely narrative', though 'robust',
According to this scholar, who never knew
What Pieter Snayers saw in 1632.

AT ASQEFAR

At Asqefar the German helmet
Rests like a scarecrow's bonnet
On a bare branch.
The shreds of coarse grey duffel
Hang round the gap a rifle
Left in a shallow trench.

'Much blood', said the shepherd,
Gesturing with his head
Towards the bald hillside.
A spent cartridge nestles
Among the dry thistles.
Blood long since dried.

Strange and remote, almost,
As these old figures traced
In Asqefar's cave:
There, pictured in red clay,
Odysseus comes back from Troy
Near the German's grave.

Twenty-five years since the battle
Plucked up the sand and let it settle
On the German soldier.
Far away now the living, the dead,
Disarmed, unhelmeted,
At Troy, at Asqefar.

WORM WITHIN

A souvenir from Sicily on the shelf:
A wooden doll carved out of some dark wood,
And crudely carved, for tourists. There it stood
Among the other stuff. Until one night,
Quietly reading to myself, I heard
It speak, or creak – a thin, persistent scratch,
Like the first scrape of a reluctant match,
Or unarticulated word
That made me look for it within myself

As if I talked to myself. But there it was,
Scratching and ticking, an erratic clock
Without a face, something as lifeless as rock
Until its own announcement that it shared
Our life with us. A woodworm, deep inside,
Drilled with its soft mouth through the pitch-stained wood
And like the owl presaging death of good,
Its beak closing as the dynasty died,
It held fear in those infinitesimal jaws.

So – to be practical – we must choose two ways:
Either to have some expert treat the thing
(Trivial, absurd, embarrassing)
Or throw it out, before the infection eats
The doors and floors away: this Trojan horse
In miniature could bring the whole house down,
I think to myself wildly, or a whole town . . .
Why do we do nothing, then, but let its course
Run, ticking, ticking, through our nights and days?

LESSON

In the big stockyards, where pigs, cows, and sheep
Stumble towards the steady punch that beats
All sense out of a body with one blow,
Certain old beasts are trained to lead the rest
And where they go the young ones meekly go.

Week after week these veterans show the way,
Then, turned back just in time, are led themselves
Back to the pens where their initiates wait.
The young must cram all knowledge in one day,
But the old who lead live on and educate.

THE FORESTERS ARMS

No trees in sight except thin spindly things
Giving no shelter to animal or bird,
Not worth the pruning, valueless as fuel,
Bearing no fruit or timber: concrete acreage
Stretches about, grey packaging of soil.
On the hill-gradient no sound is heard
But lorries changing gear; no beat of wings
Of hawk or owl above this global village.
A tanker pumps in someone's Special Ale.

Scragged earth, starved grass, coke litter under rain,
Low sheds and railway sidings – factories
That ease my life with things I do not need
Dictate such stuff. And in among it all,
Its sign new-painted, chrome replacing wood,
At odds with every neighbouring thing it sees,
The Foresters Arms marks out its old domain,
Deaf to the echo of a horn's long call
And sounds of men with axes felling trees.

TWO FACES

One gets inured to having the wrong face.
For years I thought it soft, too pink and young
To match that shrewd, mature, and self-possessed
Person behind it. In a forced grimace

I saw all that I *should* have been, the strong
Line linking nose to mouth, the net of care
Fixed by the concentration of the eyes.
Such marks upon the lineaments expressed
Things that I wanted most, but would not dare,
Prevented by the innocence I despised.

Yet now, this morning, as I change a blade,
Look up and clear the glass, I recognize
Some parody of that scored, experienced man.
But this one, as I take it, seems afraid
Of what he sees, is hesitant, with his eyes
Shifting away from something at my back.
No, this is not the one I recognized
Proleptically in mirrors; neither can
He any longer see what firm lines track
Back to that innocence he once despised.

CALLED FOR

Tonight we drive back late from talk and supper
Across miles of unlit roads, flat field and fen,
Towards home; but on the way must make a detour
And rescue you from what, half-laughingly,
We think of as your temporary world –
Some group or other, all outlandishly
Named and rigged up in fancy dress and loud
With adolescent grief. Well, we're too old
For alien caperings like that. The road
Runs towards home and habit, milk and bed.

That unborn child I locked up in neat stanzas
Survives in two or three anthologies,
An effigy sealed off from chance or changes.
Now I arrive near midnight, but too early
To claim you seventeen years afterwards:
A darkened auditorium, lit fitfully
By dizzy crimsons, pulsing and fading blues
Through which electric howls and snarled-out words
Isolate you (though only in my eyes)
Sitting among three hundred sprawling bodies.

Your pale face for a second looms up through
The jerking filters, splatterings of colour
As if spawned by the music, red and blue
Over and over – there, your face again,
Not seeing me, not seeing anything,
Distinct and separate, suddenly plain
Among so many others, strangers. Smoke
Lifts as from a winter field, obscuring
All but your face, consuming, as I look,
That child I gave protective rhetoric.

Not just this place, the tribal lights, the passive
Communion of noise and being young,
Not just the strident music which I give
No more than half an ear to; but the sense
Of drifting out into another plane
Beyond the one I move on, and moved once
To bring you into being – that is why
I falter as I call you by your name,
Claim you, as drifting up towards me now
You smile at me, ready for us to go.

Sources and Acknowledgements

Thanks are due to the authors, their representatives and publishers mentioned in the following list for their kind permission to reproduce copyright material:

Patricia Beer: 'Ghost', 'The Tale', from *Loss of the Magyar and Other Poems* (Longmans, Green & Co. Ltd); 'Love Song', 'Witch', from *The Survivors* (Longmans, Green & Co. Ltd); 'The Postilion has been Struck by Lightning', 'Four Years After', 'The Clock', 'Armistice Day', 'Concert at Long Melford Church', 'Summer Song for Me and My Aunts', 'The Chemist's Dream', 'Young Widow', 'Abbey Tomb', 'A Dream of Hanging', from *Just Like the Resurrection* (Macmillan and Co. Ltd and Macmillan Company of Canada Ltd); 'The Estuary', 'Christmas Eve', 'One Man One Vote', 'The Branch Line', 'Arms', 'The Killing of Sparrows', 'Picture of Workers Resting', from *The Estuary* (Macmillan and Co. Ltd and Macmillan Company of Canada Ltd); 'After Death', 'Female, Extinct'.

Arthur J. Bull: 'The Windmill' from *Winter Crop* (Outposts Publications); 'Nature', 'The Wind', 'Richness', 'The Acorn', 'February Thaw', 'Tastes', 'The New Coventry Cathedral', 'On the Fen', 'The Desert', 'Sargon', 'The Enemies', 'Severity', from *Selected Poems* (Outposts Publications); 'Samarkand', 'His Theology', 'Collector's Note', 'Study in Punctuation', 'Quatrain', 'Deinosaurs', 'The Bureaucrat', 'November', 'This and That', from *Century* (Outposts Publications); 'The Jungle', 'Modernismus'.

D. J. Enright: 'Warm Protest', 'Pitchfork Department', from *Addictions* (Chatto and Windus Ltd); 'The Hard Core', 'The Monuments of Hiroshima', 'Am Steinplatz', 'No Offence', from *Selected Poems* (Chatto and Windus Ltd); 'Streets', 'Children Killed in the War', 'In the Jungle', 'The Sensitive Philanthropist', 'Means Test', 'Terminal', 'Along the River', from *Daughters of the Earth* (Chatto and Windus Ltd); 'Training', 'Sunday', 'Spoilt', 'Large Mercies', 'Two Bad Things in Infant School', 'And Two Good Things', 'Always Learning', 'Insurance', 'Ugly Neck', from *The Terrible Shears: A Sequence* – Scenes from a Twenties Childhood (Chatto and Windus Ltd).

Seamus Heaney: 'Blackberry-Picking', 'Churning Day', 'Follower', 'The Diviner', 'Docker', 'The Barn', 'Personal Helicon', from *Death of a Naturalist* (Faber and Faber Ltd); 'Thatcher', 'The Wife's Tale', 'Whinlands', 'Shoreline', 'Bogland', from *Door into the Dark* (Faber and Faber Ltd); 'Serenades', 'Limbo', 'Anahorish', 'The Tollund Man', from *Wintering Out* (Faber and Faber Ltd); 'Bog Queen' (*The Listener*).

Robert Morgan: 'Valley', 'Huw's Farm', 'The Cwm above Penrhiwceiber', 'Blood Donor', 'Derelict Valley', 'The Art Lesson', 'Dickens Characters', from *The Night's Prison*; 'Black Railings', 'Champion', 'Birth of a Poet', 'The Strangers', 'The Choice', from *The Storm* (Christopher Davies); 'Men in Black', from

Poems and Extracts (University of Exeter); 'Free Coal', 'Book of Stones', 'Nightwatchman', 'Asylum for War Victims'.

Leslie Norris: 'A February Morning', 'The Ballad of Billy Rose', 'Buzzard', 'Last Leaves', 'Curlew', 'Midwinter', 'Nightingales', from *Finding Gold* (Chatto and Windus Ltd); 'Water', 'Early Frost', 'A Girl's Song', 'Owls', 'October in the Lane', from *Ransoms* (Chatto and Windus Ltd); 'July the Seventh', 'A Small War', 'Barn Owl', from *Mountains Polecats Pheasants* (Chatto and Windus Ltd).

Vernon Scannell: 'Nettles', 'Jailbird', 'Horror Film', 'The Bombing of the Café de Paris 1941', 'Mastering the Craft', from *Mastering the Craft* (Pergamon Press); 'Gunpowder Plot', 'Old Man's Song', 'Remembrance Day', 'The Jealous Wife', 'Incendiary', 'Autobiographical Note', 'Autumn', 'Walking Wounded', 'Epithets of War – I: August 1914', 'Epithets of War – III: Casualties', 'Uncle Edward's Affliction', 'Wife Killer', from *Selected Poems* (Allison and Busby Ltd); 'Legs', 'Here and Human', 'End of a Season', 'Picnic on the Lawn', 'Battlefields', from *The Winter Man* (Allison and Busby Ltd).

Anthony Thwaite: 'The Barrow', from *The Owl in the Tree* (Oxford University Press); 'At Dunwich', 'Lesson', 'Cleaning a Coin', 'Two Faces', 'Arabic Script', 'Ali Ben Shufti', 'At Asqefar', from *The Stones of Emptiness* (Oxford University Press); 'Monologue in the Valley of the Kings', 'The Foresters Arms', 'At Dunkeswell Abbey', 'Switzerland', 'Soldiers Plundering a Village', 'Worm Within', 'Entry', 'Inscriptions', from *Inscriptions* (Oxford University Press); 'Called For' (*Encounter*).